Automation
Complete Self-Assessment Guid

The guidance in this Self-Assessment is b~~ased on Automation best~~ practices and standards in business process architecture, design and quality management. The guidance is also based on the professional judgment of the individual collaborators listed in the Acknowledgments.

Notice of rights

Trademarks

Table of Contents

About The Art of Service

The Art of Service, Business Process Architects since 2000, is dedicated to helping stakeholders achieve excellence.

Defining, designing, creating, and implementing a process to solve a stakeholders challenge or meet an objective is the most valuable role… In EVERY group, company, organization and department.

Unless you're talking a one-time, single-use project, there should be a process. Whether that process is managed and implemented by humans, AI, or a combination of the two, it needs to be designed by someone with a complex enough perspective to ask the right questions.

Someone capable of asking the right questions and step back and say, 'What are we really trying to accomplish here? And is there a different way to look at it?'

With The Art of Service's Standard Requirements Self-Assessments, we empower people who can do just that — whether their title is marketer, entrepreneur, manager, salesperson, consultant, Business Process Manager, executive assistant, IT Manager, CIO etc… —they are the people who rule the future. They are people who watch the process as it happens, and ask the right questions to make the process work better.

Contact us when you need any support with this Self-Assessment and any help with templates, blue-prints and examples of standard documents you might need:

http://theartofservice.com
service@theartofservice.com

Acknowledgments

This checklist was developed under the auspices of The Art of Service, chaired by Gerardus Blokdyk.

Representatives from several client companies participated in the preparation of this Self-Assessment.

In addition, we are thankful for the design and printing services provided.

Included Resources - how to access

Included with your purchase of the book is the Automation Self-Assessment Spreadsheet Dashboard which contains all questions and Self-Assessment areas and auto-generates insights, graphs, and project RACI planning - all with examples to get you started right away.

How? Simply send an email to
access@theartofservice.com
with this books' title in the subject to get the Automation Self Assessment Tool right away.

You will receive the following contents with New and Updated specific criteria:

- The latest quick edition of the book in PDF

- The latest complete edition of the book in PDF, which criteria correspond to the criteria in...

- The Self-Assessment Excel Dashboard, and...

- Example pre-filled Self-Assessment Excel Dashboard to get familiar with results generation

- In-depth specific Checklists covering the topic

- Project management checklists and templates to assist with implementation

INCLUDES LIFETIME SELF ASSESSMENT UPDATES

Every self assessment comes with Lifetime Updates and Lifetime Free Updated Books. Lifetime Updates is an industry-first feature which allows you to receive verified self assessment updates, ensuring you always have the most accurate information at your fingertips.

Get it now- you will be glad you did - do it now, before you forget.

Send an email to **access@theartofservice.com** with this books' title in the subject to get the Automation Self Assessment Tool right away.

Your feedback is invaluable to us

If you recently bought this book, we would love to hear from you! You can do this by writing a review on amazon (or the online store where you purchased this book) about your last purchase! As part of our continual service improvement process, we love to hear real client experiences and feedback.

How does it work?
To post a review on Amazon, just log in to your account and click on the Create Your Own Review button (under Customer Reviews) of the relevant product page. You can find examples of product reviews in Amazon. If you purchased from another online store, simply follow their procedures.

What happens when I submit my review?
Once you have submitted your review, send us an email at review@theartofservice.com with the link to your review so we can properly thank you for your feedback.

Purpose of this Self-Assessment

This Self-Assessment has been developed to improve understanding of the requirements and elements of Automation, based on best practices and standards in business process architecture, design and quality management.

It is designed to allow for a rapid Self-Assessment to determine how closely existing management practices and procedures correspond to the elements of the Self-Assessment.

The criteria of requirements and elements of Automation have been rephrased in the format of a Self-Assessment questionnaire, with a seven-criterion scoring system, as explained in this document.

In this format, even with limited background knowledge of

Automation, a manager can quickly review existing operations to determine how they measure up to the standards. This in turn can serve as the starting point of a 'gap analysis' to identify management tools or system elements that might usefully be implemented in the organization to help improve overall performance.

How to use the Self-Assessment

On the following pages are a series of questions to identify to what extent your Automation initiative is complete in comparison to the requirements set in standards.

To facilitate answering the questions, there is a space in front of each question to enter a score on a scale of '1' to '5'.

1 Strongly Disagree

2 Disagree

3 Neutral

4 Agree

5 Strongly Agree

Read the question and rate it with the following in front of mind:

'In my belief,
the answer to this question is clearly defined'.

There are two ways in which you can choose to interpret this statement;

1. how aware are you that the answer to the question is clearly defined
2. for more in-depth analysis you can choose to gather

evidence and confirm the answer to the question. This obviously will take more time, most Self-Assessment users opt for the first way to interpret the question and dig deeper later on based on the outcome of the overall Self-Assessment.

A score of '1' would mean that the answer is not clear at all, where a '5' would mean the answer is crystal clear and defined. Leave emtpy when the question is not applicable or you don't want to answer it, you can skip it without affecting your score. Write your score in the space provided.

After you have responded to all the appropriate statements in each section, compute your average score for that section, using the formula provided, and round to the nearest tenth. Then transfer to the corresponding spoke in the Automation Scorecard on the second next page of the Self-Assessment.

Your completed Automation Scorecard will give you a clear presentation of which Automation areas need attention.

Automation Scorecard Example

Example of how the finalized Scorecard can look like:

Automation Scorecard

Your Scores:

BEGINNING OF THE SELF-ASSESSMENT:

CRITERION #1: RECOGNIZE

INTENT: Be aware of the need for change. Recognize that there is an unfavorable variation, problem or symptom.

In my belief, the answer to this question is clearly defined:

5 Strongly Agree

4 Agree

3 Neutral

2 Disagree

1 Strongly Disagree

1. What kinds of issues might you have when picking stories from a stack of user stories?
<--- Score

2. How are the Automation's objectives aligned to the group's overall stakeholder strategy?
<--- Score

3. What is the effect of preventative maintenance?

<--- Score

4. Do you need a fully integrated marketing automation system to support you?
<--- Score

5. What problems are you facing and how do you consider Automation will circumvent those obstacles?
<--- Score

6. What are the expected benefits of Automation to the stakeholder?
<--- Score

7. What is the Problem with Capture/Replay?
<--- Score

8. What other tools will your marketing automation system need to integrate with?
<--- Score

9. What types of problems/tasks are addressed by recommender systems applied to testing domain?
<--- Score

10. What are the minority interests and what amount of minority interests can be recognized?
<--- Score

11. To what extent does each concerned units management team recognize Automation as an effective investment?
<--- Score

12. Do you have a backlog of legacy integration needs creating bottlenecks on your path to better

customer satisfaction and greater operational efficiency?

<--- Score

13. Are employees recognized or rewarded for performance that demonstrates the highest levels of integrity?

<--- Score

14. What issues should be account for in the guidance?

<--- Score

15. Does it meet your testing needs?

<--- Score

16. What does Automation success mean to the stakeholders?

<--- Score

17. As a sponsor, customer or management, how important is it to meet goals, objectives?

<--- Score

18. What would happen if Automation weren't done?

<--- Score

19. What are the current systems in place that need to interact with the automation system?

<--- Score

20. What is needed to manage multichannel marketing campaigns and one-to-one interactions with customers around the clock?

<--- Score

21. Does Automation create potential expectations in other areas that need to be recognized and considered?

<--- Score

22. What kind of capacity is needed?

<--- Score

23. Are there recognized Automation problems?

<--- Score

24. Why do you need marketing automation?

<--- Score

25. To what extent does management recognize Automation as a tool to increase the results?

<--- Score

26. Is the need for organizational change recognized?

<--- Score

27. What problems did you encounter?

<--- Score

28. Who else hopes to benefit from it?

<--- Score

29. What information do you need to be sure is being logged in order to help identify problems?

<--- Score

30. Are there any specific expectations or concerns about the Automation team, Automation itself?

<--- Score

31. Are Automation changes recognized early enough to be approved through the regular process?

<--- Score

32. To what level do you need to disengage. Would it require full disassociation or partial?

<--- Score

33. What practices helps your organization to develop its capacity to recognize patterns?

<--- Score

34. How do you determine what other tests you need?

<--- Score

35. How do you prevent loss of organizational knowledge?

<--- Score

36. How many testers do you need?

<--- Score

37. What are the stakeholder objectives to be achieved with Automation?

<--- Score

38. Will a response program recognize when a crisis occurs and provide some level of response?

<--- Score

39. How can it meet the business needs in a streamlined fashion?

<--- Score

40. When a Automation manager recognizes a problem, what options are available?

<--- Score

41. What applications need to be integrated?

<--- Score

42. Does it include the features you need?

<--- Score

43. How many environments do you need?

<--- Score

44. Are controls defined to recognize and contain problems?

<--- Score

45. Why does automation support your business needs?

<--- Score

46. What is it that managers need to do regarding automation?

<--- Score

47. What are the talent and recruitment issues that keeps you up at night?

<--- Score

48. Is it necessary to prevent access to the production environment?

<--- Score

49. What technologies do you need?

<--- Score

50. How much are sponsors, customers, partners, stakeholders involved in Automation? In other words, what are the risks, if Automation does not deliver successfully?

<--- Score

51. What is the magnitude of overlapping automation needs in other testing groups?

<--- Score

52. To what extent would your organization benefit from being recognized as a award recipient?

<--- Score

53. How are you going to measure success?

<--- Score

54. How can end-users access the web in a way that meets their needs?

<--- Score

55. What kind of tool chain do you need?

<--- Score

56. Should you invest in industry-recognized qualifications?

<--- Score

57. Have the staff that will be involved in the project been identified?

<--- Score

58. If this component fails, what are the consequences or severity of the problems it creates?

<--- Score

59. What do you need to do to make sure that it is implemented correctly?
<--- Score

60. How much automation does your organizations customer service operation need?
<--- Score

61. Has a Manual Workaround been identified for this function?
<--- Score

62. What are your organizational capacities and capabilities needed to embrace RPA?
<--- Score

63. What is needed to actually manage multichannel marketing campaigns and one-to-one interactions with customers around the clock?
<--- Score

64. How much implementation time will you need to invest to get this up and running?
<--- Score

65. Must or should you delete/destroy personal information as soon as you no longer need it?
<--- Score

66. Can management personnel recognize the monetary benefit of Automation?
<--- Score

67. What are the key issues with e-commerce and

m-commerce?

<--- Score

68. Whose input do you need?

<--- Score

69. Do you need an RPA experienced advisor, provider, or recruiter?

<--- Score

70. What are the guidelines for effective brand-building events and experiences in your organization?

<--- Score

71. How do you stay flexible and focused to recognize larger Automation results?

<--- Score

72. If you have designed manual workarounds in the event of a robotic failure, are you prepared if the responsible humans leave?

<--- Score

73. Play nicely. what are the current systems in place that need to interact with the automation system?

<--- Score

74. What situation(s) led to this Automation Self Assessment?

<--- Score

75. Does it meet your business needs?

<--- Score

76. Compatibility: does the tool work with the particular technology that you need to test?
<--- Score

77. What information needs to be more current?
<--- Score

78. Why do you need cognitive automation?
<--- Score

Add up total points for this section:
_ _ _ _ _ = Total points for this section

Divided by: _ _ _ _ _ _ (number of statements answered) = _ _ _ _ _ _
Average score for this section

Transfer your score to the Automation Index at the beginning of the Self-Assessment.

CRITERION #2: DEFINE:

INTENT: Formulate the stakeholder problem. Define the problem, needs and objectives.

In my belief, the answer to this question is clearly defined:

5 Strongly Agree

4 Agree

3 Neutral

2 Disagree

1 Strongly Disagree

1. Is Automation linked to key stakeholder goals and objectives?
<--- Score

2. Will team members perform Automation work when assigned and in a timely fashion?
<--- Score

3. Has the direction changed at all during the course

of Automation? If so, when did it change and why?
<--- Score

4. Has the improvement team collected the 'voice of the customer' (obtained feedback – qualitative and quantitative)?
<--- Score

5. Are team charters developed?
<--- Score

6. Has your organization defined the specific type of water required for each of its testing procedures?
<--- Score

7. What would be the goal or target for a Automation's improvement team?
<--- Score

8. When is/was the Automation start date?
<--- Score

9. Are different versions of process maps needed to account for the different types of inputs?
<--- Score

10. Does the team have regular meetings?
<--- Score

11. Who are the Automation improvement team members, including Management Leads and Coaches?
<--- Score

12. What are the reliability requirements?

<--- Score

13. Have the customer needs been translated into specific, measurable requirements? How?
<--- Score

14. What are the performance requirements?
<--- Score

15. How is the team tracking and documenting its work?
<--- Score

16. Has a project plan, Gantt chart, or similar been developed/completed?
<--- Score

17. Has the Automation work been fairly and/ or equitably divided and delegated among team members who are qualified and capable to perform the work? Has everyone contributed?
<--- Score

18. If substitutes have been appointed, have they been briefed on the Automation goals and received regular communications as to the progress to date?
<--- Score

19. Is there a critical path to deliver Automation results?
<--- Score

20. How do test and QA managers make a business case for functions?
<--- Score

21. Is a fully trained team formed, supported, and committed to work on the Automation improvements?
<--- Score

22. What are barriers to success in creating a valid business case?
<--- Score

23. How much it support is required for making changes?
<--- Score

24. Are there any constraints known that bear on the ability to perform Automation work? How is the team addressing them?
<--- Score

25. Are customer(s) identified and segmented according to their different needs and requirements?
<--- Score

26. Is the team formed and are team leaders (Coaches and Management Leads) assigned?
<--- Score

27. Is Automation currently on schedule according to the plan?
<--- Score

28. Is there a completed, verified, and validated high-level 'as is' (not 'should be' or 'could be') stakeholder process map?
<--- Score

29. What key stakeholder process output measure(s)

does Automation leverage and how?
<--- Score

30. How did the Automation manager receive input to the development of a Automation improvement plan and the estimated completion dates/times of each activity?
<--- Score

31. Which are requirements workflow tasks done in the elaboration phase?
<--- Score

32. Is there a Automation management charter, including stakeholder case, problem and goal statements, scope, milestones, roles and responsibilities, communication plan?
<--- Score

33. Will there be other use cases from a marketing outreach perspective for sending communication to customers?
<--- Score

34. If you are tracking the number of the lines of code and the cyclomatic complexity of the test automation code, what type of metric are you gathering?
<--- Score

35. Is there a completed SIPOC representation, describing the Suppliers, Inputs, Process, Outputs, and Customers?
<--- Score

36. What customer feedback methods were used to

solicit their input?
<--- Score

37. If you are tracking the frequency with which the test automation code reports a defect that is not really a defect, what metric are you gathering?
<--- Score

38. Has everyone on the team, including the team leaders, been properly trained?
<--- Score

39. Is the team sponsored by a champion or stakeholder leader?
<--- Score

40. How often are the team meetings?
<--- Score

41. What is your organizations definition of turnaround time?
<--- Score

42. Is the Automation scope manageable?
<--- Score

43. Can the test sequence of actions be defined?
<--- Score

44. What are the rough order estimates on cost savings/opportunities that Automation brings?
<--- Score

45. How will variation in the actual durations of each activity be dealt with to ensure that the expected Automation results are met?

<--- Score

46. Will team members regularly document their Automation work?
<--- Score

47. Has anyone else (internal or external to the group) attempted to solve this problem or a similar one before? If so, what knowledge can be leveraged from these previous efforts?
<--- Score

48. Do the requirements determine the level of automation?
<--- Score

49. Is the current 'as is' process being followed? If not, what are the discrepancies?
<--- Score

50. Is the improvement team aware of the different versions of a process: what they think it is vs. what it actually is vs. what it should be vs. what it could be?
<--- Score

51. What are the compelling stakeholder reasons for embarking on Automation?
<--- Score

52. Do you also desire / require outbound automation with SMS or email?
<--- Score

53. Has a team charter been developed and communicated?
<--- Score

54. Are there different segments of customers?
<--- Score

55. What are the boundaries of the scope? What is in bounds and what is not? What is the start point? What is the stop point?
<--- Score

56. How do you know you are ready to expand the scope of automation beyond RPA?
<--- Score

57. Is there regularly 100% attendance at the team meetings? If not, have appointed substitutes attended to preserve cross-functionality and full representation?
<--- Score

58. How do you keep key subject matter experts in the loop?
<--- Score

59. How does the Automation manager ensure against scope creep?
<--- Score

60. Have the roles and responsibilities - who does what - of the participants been defined?
<--- Score

61. Is the minimum hardware configuration compatible with the requirements of your organization?
<--- Score

62. Will there be several use cases from a marketing outreach perspective for sending communication to customers?
<--- Score

63. Are stakeholder processes mapped?
<--- Score

64. Is data collected and displayed to better understand customer(s) critical needs and requirements.
<--- Score

65. How do you define the market, how big is it, and how fast is it growing?
<--- Score

66. Are customers identified and high impact areas defined?
<--- Score

67. What are the security requirements for a Bot?
<--- Score

68. Is your organization subject to a legal requirement that test cases be demonstrable?
<--- Score

69. What are the dynamics of the communication plan?
<--- Score

70. Are improvement team members fully trained on Automation?
<--- Score

71. How was the 'as is' process map developed, reviewed, verified and validated?
<--- Score

72. Do you have to make it possible for nonprogrammers to create automated test cases?
<--- Score

73. What critical content must be communicated – who, what, when, where, and how?
<--- Score

74. What specifically is the problem? Where does it occur? When does it occur? What is its extent?
<--- Score

75. What adjustments will be required of your teams in order to benefit?
<--- Score

76. Has/have the customer(s) been identified?
<--- Score

77. Is the team equipped with available and reliable resources?
<--- Score

78. Has a high-level 'as is' process map been completed, verified and validated?
<--- Score

79. Is full participation by members in regularly held team meetings guaranteed?
<--- Score

80. What reporting requirements do you have?

<--- Score

81. Use cases - how do you report test coverage and where the bugs are?
<--- Score

82. Do the problem and goal statements meet the SMART criteria (specific, measurable, attainable, relevant, and time-bound)?
<--- Score

83. What are the security requirements?
<--- Score

84. How will the Automation team and the group measure complete success of Automation?
<--- Score

85. What constraints exist that might impact the team?
<--- Score

86. Is the team adequately staffed with the desired cross-functionality? If not, what additional resources are available to the team?
<--- Score

87. When are meeting minutes sent out? Who is on the distribution list?
<--- Score

88. What are the Roles and Responsibilities for each team member and its leadership? Where is this documented?
<--- Score

89. Which requirements are functional business requirements?

<--- Score

90. When is the estimated completion date?
<--- Score

91. How do you define acceptance criteria for state-of-the-art characteristics?

<--- Score

92. What basic physical requirements must be in place when installing computer equipment in your organisation?

<--- Score

Add up total points for this section:
_____ = Total points for this section

Divided by: _____ (number of
statements answered) = _____
Average score for this section

Transfer your score to the Automation
Index at the beginning of the Self-
Assessment.

CRITERION #3: MEASURE:

INTENT: Gather the correct data. Measure the current performance and evolution of the situation.

In my belief, the answer to this question is clearly defined:

5 Strongly Agree

4 Agree

3 Neutral

2 Disagree

1 Strongly Disagree

1. Are high impact defects defined and identified in the stakeholder process?
<--- Score

2. How long does it take to analyze campaign data across all marketing channels without a marketing automation system?
<--- Score

3. When the system under development is a new system what analysis strategy do you use?

<--- Score

4. How do you prioritize by modelling out the practices and processes in scope for RPA?

<--- Score

5. Is long term and short term variability accounted for?

<--- Score

6. Are process variation components displayed/ communicated using suitable charts, graphs, plots?

<--- Score

7. Which analysis strategies incurs the highest risk yet has the potential to provide high value to the business?

<--- Score

8. How do you measure the effectiveness of your marketing?

<--- Score

9. Should you outsource and/ or offshore repetitive tasks to a less cost-prohibitive (but potentially more errorprone) workforce?

<--- Score

10. How will you ensure impacted stakeholders understand the what, why, and how of automation?

<--- Score

11. What particular quality tools did the team find

helpful in establishing measurements?
<--- Score

12. What impact will automation have on your people and culture?
<--- Score

13. Inherent Risk Likelihood and Impact. In the absence of controls, how likely is the fraud risk and what would the impact be if it were to occur?
<--- Score

14. What is the impact of automation on care?
<--- Score

15. What is the current labor cost of the process?
<--- Score

16. What impact will automating functions currently carried out by humans have on society, on the economy, and on the way your organization approaches opportunity?
<--- Score

17. Was a data collection plan established?
<--- Score

18. How would automation impact your organization operation and workflow?
<--- Score

19. Is data collection planned and executed?
<--- Score

20. Is data collected on key measures that were identified?

<--- Score

21. Is Process Variation Displayed/Communicated?
<--- Score

22. What are the agreed upon definitions of the high impact areas, defect(s), unit(s), and opportunities that will figure into the process capability metrics?
<--- Score

23. Is there a Performance Baseline?
<--- Score

24. What should goals, objectives and priorities are established for your IT automation project?
<--- Score

25. Who participated in the data collection for measurements?
<--- Score

26. How are potential projects prioritized?
<--- Score

27. What charts has the team used to display the components of variation in the process?
<--- Score

28. How will rpa impact roles and responsibilities?
<--- Score

29. What are your use cases and how are they applied to analyze the requirements of the system?
<--- Score

30. Is key measure data collection planned and executed, process variation displayed and communicated and performance baselined?
<--- Score

31. Will this have an impact on the headcount?
<--- Score

32. What key issues arise when considering your organizations goals, objectives and priorities for automation?
<--- Score

33. Do the automated scripts verify the behavior of the client; did the correct window appear and did any results appear?
<--- Score

34. What is the cost for providing future system enhancements?
<--- Score

35. What external factors influence the analytics technology domain and how are corresponding evolving?
<--- Score

36. What impact has RPA had on your workforce?
<--- Score

37. What are the key input variables? What are the key process variables? What are the key output variables?
<--- Score

38. What has the team done to assure the stability and accuracy of the measurement process?

<--- Score

39. How does cause or corporate societal marketing affect your personal consumer behavior?
<--- Score

40. How will you manage change that will cause the robots to malfunction?
<--- Score

41. How does your organization verify manual and automated result entry?
<--- Score

42. Are you sufficiently leveraging the data being produced by OT and IoT systems for smarter analytics, improved process automation, better use of resources and predictive maintenance?
<--- Score

43. Where is the program focusing its fraud risk management activities?
<--- Score

44. Are key measures identified and agreed upon?
<--- Score

45. What are the key performance metrics that you use to measure projects and investments?
<--- Score

46. Is lines of code a good measure of effort in effort-aware models?
<--- Score

47. What pieces of the product and architecture are highest priority and why?

<--- Score

48. Does organization automation for the preanalytical phase improve data quality?

<--- Score

49. Is this a priority project?

<--- Score

50. Does the tool control access to risk analysis data (e.g., logon/password encryption)?

<--- Score

51. How are you forecasting the impacts: what are the various forecasts of how automation will transform business?

<--- Score

52. Robotic process automation growth: what function will be most impacted?

<--- Score

53. How do you measure the payback from advertising, sales promotion, and public relations?

<--- Score

54. What are the primary obstacles to your organization achieving more F&A business impact through digital?

<--- Score

55. What physical security measures are in place?

<--- Score

56. Is a test worth five times more because it is run on five systems instead of one?

<--- Score

57. What measures assess your organizations RPA performance and impact on workforce development?

<--- Score

58. How can you maintain margins while enduring intense price pressure and spiraling costs?

<--- Score

59. What data was collected (past, present, future/ongoing)?

<--- Score

60. Have you found any 'ground fruit' or 'low-hanging fruit' for immediate remedies to the gap in performance?

<--- Score

61. Will IT operations analytics platforms replace your APM suites?

<--- Score

62. At what level of production will cost savings associated with automation start to drive overall cost to the materials cost level?

<--- Score

63. What information-gathering strategy enables the analyst to see the reality of the situation rather than listen to others describe it?

<--- Score

64. Does rpa drive down costs while improving performance and efficiency in your organization, how do yo know, what are your measurements?
<--- Score

65. Is a solid data collection plan established that includes measurement systems analysis?
<--- Score

66. Are the results of the analysis well presented?
<--- Score

67. What key measures identified indicate the performance of the stakeholder process?
<--- Score

68. Do you analyze your data and reporting on KPIs and ROI?
<--- Score

69. How large is the gap between current performance and the customer-specified (goal) performance?
<--- Score

70. What impact will automation have on your security and compliance?
<--- Score

71. Is sustainability an opportunity or cost?
<--- Score

72. What is the psychological and social impact of automation on metadata creators?
<--- Score

73. Do you need a centralized view of analytics or audit or are you reliant on an individual to confirm and trigger a process?

<--- Score

74. How do you ensure software quality in a cost effective way?

<--- Score

75. What cost size of cost saving do you require from Robotic Process Automation?

<--- Score

Add up total points for this section:

_ _ _ _ _ = Total points for this section

Divided by: _ _ _ _ _ _ (number of statements answered) = _ _ _ _ _ _
Average score for this section

Transfer your score to the Automation Index at the beginning of the Self-Assessment.

CRITERION #4: ANALYZE:

INTENT: Analyze causes, assumptions and hypotheses.

In my belief, the answer to this question is clearly defined:

5 Strongly Agree

4 Agree

3 Neutral

2 Disagree

1 Strongly Disagree

1. Understand what you need to do -which processes need automation?
<--- Score

2. Given the geopolitical turmoil and advances in automation, should your organization revisit re-shoring and in-sourcing decision-making process?
<--- Score

3. Is organization data the responsibility of your

organization, or does IT have any involvement?
<--- Score

4. How should the process owners be engaged to try automation?
<--- Score

5. What are the right processes to optimize?
<--- Score

6. Why use robotic process automation?
<--- Score

7. Robotic process automation budget: who is paying?
<--- Score

8. Is artificial intelligence a threat or opportunity?
<--- Score

9. How many processes have been automated in your organization using RPA?
<--- Score

10. What role does robotic process automation play ensuring strategy success?
<--- Score

11. How can you reduce the number of errors in the name and address field on the data entry screen?
<--- Score

12. Where can robotic process automation be used?
<--- Score

13. How do you perceive AI and Robotic Process Automation?

<--- Score

14. Does the benefit of structure in the audit process derive from the automation and mechanization of judgment, or enhancing the fabric of judgment?

<--- Score

15. Are there opportunities to create simple scripts to save time and find bugs?

<--- Score

16. What do you use data for?

<--- Score

17. How can you better process documents to improve business outcomes?

<--- Score

18. Where is robotic process automation taking us?

<--- Score

19. What proportion of patch application is automated and is there an opportunity to increase automation?

<--- Score

20. How is robotic process automation different than traditional application automation ?

<--- Score

21. Robotics process automation - evolution or

revolution?

<--- Score

22. Can you give the business the data that it needs?

<--- Score

23. What are the top three inhibitors to growing Robotic Process Automation at your organization?

<--- Score

24. Is compliance established through a combination of system automation and manual processes/procedures?

<--- Score

25. Should workers fear Robotic Process Automation?

<--- Score

26. With your digital platform of tools and processes how do you get performance and profit under control?

<--- Score

27. Do you regularly assess that the configuration of the rule set and processing logic remains relevant to your business needs and demands?

<--- Score

28. Which criteria help determine if your processes are suitable to automate by means of Process Robotics?

<--- Score

29. What is robotic process automation compared

to traditional automation?
<--- Score

30. How do you exploit robotics technology to the fullest (e.g., train, repair, clean, de-bug, program for quick set-up)?
<--- Score

31. How do you manage the process?
<--- Score

32. What data do not you want?
<--- Score

33. Which process criteria are best suited to RPA?
<--- Score

34. Do you have established metrics and measurements for AI solutions and process performance that are important to and directly serve your end-users and/or stakeholders?
<--- Score

35. How do employees work alongside the digital workforce in executing a process?
<--- Score

36. What are the architectural components for your Process Robotics?
<--- Score

37. How secure is the most important component of your application: your database?
<--- Score

38. Opportunities by industry - what types

of opportunities are available from various industries?

<--- Score

39. What are your current lead management processes and where are the specific areas you would like to automate?

<--- Score

40. Customer data platform or marketing automation what do you really need?

<--- Score

41. Do robots dream of perfect processes?

<--- Score

42. Are you aware of the data breach notification laws in your organizations in which you operate?

<--- Score

43. Does the solution have process automation capabilities to automate workflows for ITSM and ITAM tasks, as well as common events, such as hotfixes or release upgrades?

<--- Score

44. What sources of information (types of data) are exploited?

<--- Score

45. How will business process and behavioral change be managed?

<--- Score

46. Review leads with high scores that did not turn into opportunities. How could the scoring be

improved?

<--- Score

47. Are there points in the process you can optimize?

<--- Score

48. Do you need a customer data platform?

<--- Score

49. Robotic process automation growth: what function will be most affected?

<--- Score

50. Where is automation in the data center headed?

<--- Score

51. When the process becomes fully automated, where lies the responsibility, accountability and, above all, the liability?

<--- Score

52. Reasons for using Robotic Process Automation Tools?

<--- Score

53. What process or interaction specifically is to be automated and why?

<--- Score

54. What kinds of desktop processes are the best for automation?

<--- Score

55. How can a Finance function prepare for

Robotic Process Automation?

<--- Score

56. What is the governance framework you use for adoption of RPA and alignment to risk, compliance and IT/data frameworks?

<--- Score

57. Required processing time for each transaction?

<--- Score

58. Why robotic process automation now?

<--- Score

59. How much data do you need?

<--- Score

60. Continuous integration is the automation of the build process?

<--- Score

61. When implementing results reporting for test automation, how do you allow the reader to make a quick assessment of the progress of the test execution?

<--- Score

62. Are you listening to the voice of your customer (VoC) and connecting that to the right metrics and processes to achieve your business objectives?

<--- Score

63. Robotic process automation: strategic transformation lever for global business services?

<--- Score

64. What techniques are used for gathering information during all three stages of the information-gathering process (As-Is, improvements, and To-Be)?
<--- Score

65. When and why is automation used in the software development process?
<--- Score

66. Opportunities by category - what types of opportunities are available by category?
<--- Score

67. What information is generated by, consumed by, processed on, stored in, and retrieved by the system?
<--- Score

68. Can the functions performed by your applications be initiated by an external process automation system?
<--- Score

69. What is the criticality / importance of the records (data) stored in the file?
<--- Score

70. What type of processes are applicable for Robotic Process Automation?
<--- Score

71. What roles and personnel are able to deliver all the details, even when moving down the pyramid levels, for business process automation?
<--- Score

72. What do you believe to be the most important components of the value proposition for Robotic Process Automation?

<--- Score

73. Requirements: Have you developed requirements including core business processes to be automated? How will business process and behavioral change be managed?

<--- Score

74. Is this a one-shot effort, or will you need to do performance testing as part of your development process for years to come?

<--- Score

75. Opportunities by type - what types of opportunities are available by type?

<--- Score

76. Why should you adopt Robotic Process Automation?

<--- Score

77. Bi automation. does the bi platform support various self-service bi automation processes that allow business users to do more with less?

<--- Score

78. Why should you be considering Robotic Process Automation?

<--- Score

79. How do you manage the security of your automated processes and prevent cyber attacks,

intrusions or hacks?

<--- Score

80. Do you feel your current IT process requires better automation?

<--- Score

81. Have many other companies are already implemented Robotic Process Automation?

<--- Score

82. Have you been able to integrate with your other key business systems, like sales force automation, to avoid rekeying data or islands of information?

<--- Score

83. What are the pain points in the current process?

<--- Score

84. Are there limits on interfacing Robotic Process Automation or AI software with your other licensed software?

<--- Score

85. Is this data available in any existing business software application?

<--- Score

86. Is your organization ready for a new model of process transformation that puts exceptional customer experiences first?

<--- Score

87. Are components of the process digitised in

order to be further automated?

<--- Score

88. Does the marketing automation system support an automated mapping of your data model?

<--- Score

89. What data is used and where does it come from?

<--- Score

90. Is there an annual membership or similar which is processed through another system?

<--- Score

91. How do your internal processes affect the end customer?

<--- Score

92. How do consumers process and evaluate your prices?

<--- Score

93. Staff need to know how to respond if something breaks down in a production setting: Is it the same kind of escalation process as when other technology fails?

<--- Score

94. Does your organization support the automation of this process?

<--- Score

95. What feedback have you received from employees that are working with Robotic Process

Automation?

<--- Score

96. How can a digital robotic workforce replace labor-intensive manual processes in your organization?

<--- Score

97. What is the role of data encryption in IoT?

<--- Score

98. Perhaps automation of the business process is required?

<--- Score

99. Are there any security risks in running business processes from a virtual delivery center?

<--- Score

100. What is the trend for Robotic Process Automation and AI adoption?

<--- Score

101. Robotic process automation can be characterised as an it-enabled business process innovation. how should robotic process automation be managed?

<--- Score

102. What is the advantage of Robotic Process Automation (Robotic Process Automation) in service management processes?

<--- Score

103. How does robotic process automation integrate into your operation?

<--- Score

104. Is the process supporting a regulated environment or activities?
<--- Score

105. What are the problems or inefficiencies encountered with the existing process/system?
<--- Score

106. How often does the storage tiering algorithm move data between tiers?
<--- Score

107. What are the methods used to identify improvement opportunities during business process automation?
<--- Score

108. In which functions do you currently use Robotic Process Automation?
<--- Score

109. What are the changes in the range of manufacturing processes/tasks that are automated?
<--- Score

110. There are so many hassles and slowdowns that Robotic Process Automation can address, who wants to wait for the improvements?
<--- Score

111. What data do you use now?
<--- Score

112. Is your business ready for robotic process automation?

<--- Score

113. Which robotic process automation software should you use?

<--- Score

114. How expensive is it to implement control access / procedural controls of records (data)?

<--- Score

115. When does robotic process automation make the biggest difference?

<--- Score

116. Do you have an opportunity to bring work back on shore, albeit to a digital workforce?

<--- Score

117. What are the necessary functional requirements or steps in the process?

<--- Score

118. Get unstuck. what are your current lead management processes and where are the speci c areas you would like to automate?

<--- Score

119. How well understood is the process?

<--- Score

120. What are the regions of the testing process that you should consider?

<--- Score

121. Roles and responsibilities: who will be accountable and responsible for activities in marketing processes?

<--- Score

122. What flooring design does the data center implement (raised floor, etc.)?

<--- Score

123. How does the innovation of software process automation fit into the view of software evolution?

<--- Score

124. What major changes are occurring in product and process technology?

<--- Score

125. Which best describes your organizations application of artificial intelligence in the automation of its processes today?

<--- Score

126. How is your organization seizing the opportunities and managing the challenges it faces regarding its people capabilities?

<--- Score

127. What are the business process flows that need to be automated across corresponding applications?

<--- Score

128. What about privacy and data protection?

<--- Score

129. What are the opportunities for robotic

automation to meet some of your needs for skilled talent?

<--- Score

130. How does the consumer process competitive brand information and make a final value judgment?

<--- Score

131. Which step in the process is most difficult to perform?

<--- Score

132. What data needs to be migrated?

<--- Score

133. Robotic process automation buying decisions: who is responsible?

<--- Score

134. If business leaders truly want to improve processes, how do they move forward?

<--- Score

135. How do you account for the purpose of an algorithm and the kind of data it uses when making automated decisions?

<--- Score

136. Robotic process automation ecosystem: what role do third parties play?

<--- Score

137. How is your organization using design thinking in the business services product development process?

<--- Score

138. Where is robotic process automation being used?
<--- Score

139. Why are you deciding to deploy it here at your organization and for this process?
<--- Score

140. Which processes would be suitable to pilot?
<--- Score

141. What do robotic process automation and ai mean for your sourcing contracts?
<--- Score

Add up total points for this section:
_____ = Total points for this section

Divided by: _____ (number of statements answered) = _____
Average score for this section

Transfer your score to the Automation Index at the beginning of the Self-Assessment.

CRITERION #5: IMPROVE:

INTENT: Develop a practical solution.
Innovate, establish and test the
solution and to measure the results.

In my belief, the answer to this
question is clearly defined:

5 Strongly Agree

4 Agree

3 Neutral

2 Disagree

1 Strongly Disagree

1. How will the group know that the solution worked?
<--- Score

**2. Do have the capability to evaluate the level of
risk that AI systems are exploited by malicious
actors and determine appropriate risk controls?**
<--- Score

3. Does your solution support public-facing

E-forms that can be filled out and submitted on line?

<--- Score

4. Are possible solutions generated and tested?

<--- Score

5. What levels and types of training are required for different staff members and other users to understand and utilise the system?

<--- Score

6. How does this solution work; for example, is it hosted on premise or is it a SaaS offering?

<--- Score

7. Is guidance needed for IT controls documentation?

<--- Score

8. Describe the design of the pilot and what tests were conducted, if any?

<--- Score

9. How are you developing the knowledge and skillsets of your teams?

<--- Score

10. Do you have quality assurance and risk management programs in place for understanding how AI systems/models must be validated and developed?

<--- Score

11. Were any criteria developed to assist the team in testing and evaluating potential solutions?

<--- Score

12. Care and feeding. As with any technology, marketing automation tools evolve. Who is going to own it and ensure that its being optimized?
<--- Score

13. What are the best-practices most suitable to your test automation problem at hand and how do you apply them in development of the automated test scripts?
<--- Score

14. Does automation bias decision-making?
<--- Score

15. What were the underlying assumptions on the cost-benefit analysis?
<--- Score

16. Is the implementation plan designed?
<--- Score

17. Are there any constraints (technical, political, cultural, or otherwise) that would inhibit certain solutions?
<--- Score

18. What is your commitment to R&D as a percentage of your total expenditure dedicated to improvements?
<--- Score

19. How does the solution remove the key sources of issues discovered in the analyze phase?
<--- Score

20. What attendant changes will need to be made to ensure that the solution is successful?

<--- Score

21. Can workflow be automated for a specific document type and workflow template?

<--- Score

22. What decisions does your organization face in designing and managing a sales force?

<--- Score

23. Was a pilot designed for the proposed solution(s)?

<--- Score

24. Is pilot data collected and analyzed?

<--- Score

25. Development has raised the level of abstraction through the use of models: are you doing the same for testing?

<--- Score

26. What communications are necessary to support the implementation of the solution?

<--- Score

27. How will the solution be deployed?

<--- Score

28. When you execute scripts that will produce the same result, what happens when you rearrange the window?

<--- Score

29. One of the hardest things to manage during the system development lifecycle is expectations. Keeping a good audit trail should help. How good are your deliverable definitions?

<--- Score

30. Is the documentation easy to use and maintain?

<--- Score

31. What types of technology solutions have you deployed in your organization?

<--- Score

32. Each of the areas will need to be developed towards the outcome that has been decided upon. How will each of corresponding activities be taken forward?

<--- Score

33. Are there effective automation solutions available to help with this?

<--- Score

34. Who owns the third-party risk management program?

<--- Score

35. Should your organization invest in cyber risk insurance?

<--- Score

36. What types of procedures are implemented, given increased globalization, to reduce risk?

<--- Score

37. Is there a cost/benefit analysis of optimal solution(s)?
<--- Score

38. What tools were most useful during the improve phase?
<--- Score

39. What are the security requirements for the development environment?
<--- Score

40. Does your organization evaluate the appropriateness of its reference intervals, and take corrective action if necessary?
<--- Score

41. Is third-party risk management integrated with your third-party management policies?
<--- Score

42. What tools were used to tap into the creativity and encourage 'outside the box' thinking?
<--- Score

43. Is the optimal solution selected based on testing and analysis?
<--- Score

44. Can your organization contract out IT Risk Management Automation's duty to warn or is it inherent and unavoidable?
<--- Score

45. Is a solution implementation plan established, including schedule/work breakdown structure,

resources, risk management plan, cost/budget, and control plan?

<--- Score

46. How can your organization improve its marketing skills?

<--- Score

47. Are improved process ('should be') maps modified based on pilot data and analysis?

<--- Score

48. Risk identification addresses the What might go wrong?

<--- Score

49. How did the team generate the list of possible solutions?

<--- Score

50. Do you look to improve service sales and service delivery consistency?

<--- Score

51. How do you decide what to automate?

<--- Score

52. What steps are required in developing an advertising program?

<--- Score

53. What type of training is offered internally to assist employees in gaining and developing own computer skills?

<--- Score

54. What is the team's contingency plan for potential problems occurring in implementation?
<--- Score

55. What does the 'should be' process map/design look like?
<--- Score

56. Do you document all corrective action taken when there is a test system failure?
<--- Score

57. Is there a small-scale pilot for proposed improvement(s)? What conclusions were drawn from the outcomes of a pilot?
<--- Score

58. Is a contingency plan established?
<--- Score

59. Do you have adequate business and IT governance frameworks in place to provide oversight, arbitrate, and render decisions regarding AI-enabled solutions?
<--- Score

60. Are policies and procedures documented and adequate for the safe handling of electrical equipment?
<--- Score

61. How does your organization go about selecting the marketing automation solution that best suits needs?
<--- Score

62. Are the best solutions selected?
<--- Score

63. How will the team or the process owner(s) monitor the implementation plan to see that it is working as intended?
<--- Score

64. Are you addressing the business continuity risk?
<--- Score

65. Which risks poses the greatest threat to your organizations growth?
<--- Score

66. What are influential macroenvironment developments for your organization?
<--- Score

67. How does your organization determine who is authorized to receive results?
<--- Score

68. Are new and improved process ('should be') maps developed?
<--- Score

69. How do you improve customer engagement with social media?
<--- Score

70. Is automation preferred as a result of environmental conditions?
<--- Score

71. What decisions does your organization face in managing channels?

<--- Score

72. How does globalization play a part in increased risk?

<--- Score

73. With existing staff, how long will it take to develop/ maintain/enhance specific automated methods at each site independently?

<--- Score

74. How do you reduce the risk?

<--- Score

75. How can manufacturing improvement techniques such as lean and Six Sigma be used to improve quality in your automated laboratories?

<--- Score

76. What is the implementation plan?

<--- Score

77. Is the emphasis on developmental or operational testing?

<--- Score

78. What service level measures will you use to account for new service delivery method and commitments for improvements in quality and efficiency?

<--- Score

79. Can digital tools optimize design and engineering phases?

<--- Score

80. What is third-party risk management & third-party due diligence?
<--- Score

81. What is Automation's impact on utilizing the best solution(s)?
<--- Score

82. What are digitalisation and automation experiences within risk management?
<--- Score

83. What are measurable indicators for the efficiency of the documentation task in the lab?
<--- Score

84. How do consumers make purchasing decisions?
<--- Score

85. Schedule: is the schedule realistic and can the budget be mapped to the schedule?
<--- Score

86. Understanding algorithm aversion: When is advice from automation discounted?
<--- Score

87. What tools were used to evaluate the potential solutions?
<--- Score

88. Can the tool documentation cover screen capture/compare etc (needed for audit purposes)?

<--- Score

89. Which of your projects is best suited for a pilot project for the test automation tool?
<--- Score

90. What challenges does your organization face in developing new products and services?
<--- Score

91. How do you prepare the automation roadmap?
<--- Score

92. Which Fusion Middleware products are used in your solution?
<--- Score

93. How does implementing a testing automation strategy improve quality assurance for web-based applications?
<--- Score

94. What lessons, if any, from a pilot were incorporated into the design of the full-scale solution?
<--- Score

95. How is testing different in Agile software development?
<--- Score

96. How do you continue developing knowledge and skillsets?
<--- Score

97. How can you deliver the insights needed to make informed business decisions?

<--- Score

98. That there are numerous ways that automation solution tools can integrate with your applications. Which way is best for your organization?
<--- Score

99. What error proofing will be done to address some of the discrepancies observed in the 'as is' process?
<--- Score

Add up total points for this section:
_____ = Total points for this section

Divided by: _____ (number of statements answered) = _____
Average score for this section

Transfer your score to the Automation Index at the beginning of the Self-Assessment.

CRITERION #6: CONTROL:

INTENT: Implement the practical solution. Maintain the performance and correct possible complications.

In my belief, the answer to this question is clearly defined:

5 Strongly Agree

4 Agree

3 Neutral

2 Disagree

1 Strongly Disagree

1. How do you plan to increase automation capabilities in the future?
<--- Score

2. What control standards should apply to RPA?
<--- Score

3. What is your risk mitigation plan?
<--- Score

4. What should the next improvement project be that is related to Automation?

<--- Score

5. Does your organization have all the source code for the applications under good configuration control at present?

<--- Score

6. Who will manage and monitor the software robot?

<--- Score

7. Will any special training be provided for results interpretation?

<--- Score

8. Does your organization employ a quality control system?

<--- Score

9. What is the control/monitoring plan?

<--- Score

10. Are the internal controls designed and managed in a continuous basis or is it reactive?

<--- Score

11. What is the most likely area of the test automation to fail and how do you monitor to make sure it is not failing?

<--- Score

12. Are documented procedures clear and easy to follow for the operators?

<--- Score

13. Has the improved process and its steps been standardized?
<--- Score

14. Are there documented procedures?
<--- Score

15. Is knowledge gained on process shared and institutionalized?
<--- Score

16. Is there documentation that will support the successful operation of the improvement?
<--- Score

17. How can robotics, natural language systems, and learning systems be classified?
<--- Score

18. Is there a standardized process?
<--- Score

19. Who is responsible for activating the plan?
<--- Score

20. How will input, process, and output variables be checked to detect for sub-optimal conditions?
<--- Score

21. Is a response plan established and deployed?
<--- Score

22. Is execution aligned with design standards?
<--- Score

23. Is the right technology used for managing internal controls?

<--- Score

24. Is new knowledge gained imbedded in the response plan?

<--- Score

25. What is the recommended frequency of auditing?

<--- Score

26. How fast does your organization move to implement and scale digital workforce, when the benefits from robotic process automation are high and the payback period is so attractive, at just under one year?

<--- Score

27. How do you monitor performance and embed IA goals in performance management to ensure value?

<--- Score

28. Which aspects of consumer behavior does your organization marketing plan emphasize and why?

<--- Score

29. What are the metrics you plan to baseline against in order to understand whether or not the returns of a marketing automation platform make sense?

<--- Score

30. Are your processes mission critical like regulatory compliance standards that require

full visibility and traceability of every action and decision within a process such as: PCI, HIPAA and SOX?
<--- Score

31. Is there a control plan in place for sustaining improvements (short and long-term)?
<--- Score

32. What are the critical parameters to watch?
<--- Score

33. Are the room temperature and humidity adequately controlled in all seasons?
<--- Score

34. Have you explored what sorts of gains in productivity, efficiency and waste reduction could be achieved by deploying robots in your operations?
<--- Score

35. Does the Automation performance meet the customer's requirements?
<--- Score

36. Do you want only authorized users to access and edit automations and control execution?
<--- Score

37. Are there plans (or considerations) to increase the emphasis on marketing?
<--- Score

38. How will the day-to-day responsibilities for monitoring and continual improvement be

transferred from the improvement team to the process owner?

<--- Score

39. Does your approach scale to realistic GUI applications?

<--- Score

40. How will report readings be checked to effectively monitor performance?

<--- Score

41. What key inputs and outputs are being measured on an ongoing basis?

<--- Score

42. How easy is it to write tests against the selected interface?

<--- Score

43. Which it general controls should be tested?

<--- Score

44. How does your organization plan for and effectively manage the surges in data?

<--- Score

45. How important do you expect workforce capabilities to be in supporting your organizations future growth plans?

<--- Score

46. What is the planned response time to fill the customers needs?

<--- Score

47. How will new or emerging customer needs/ requirements be checked/communicated to orient the process toward meeting the new specifications and continually reducing variation?
<--- Score

48. Who is the Automation process owner?
<--- Score

49. Would guidance be useful on the timing of management testing of controls?
<--- Score

50. How does your organization screen and monitor third parties?
<--- Score

51. Measure everything. what are the metrics you plan to baseline against in order to understand whether or not the returns of a marketing automation platform make sense?
<--- Score

52. Is there a recommended audit plan for routine surveillance inspections of Automation's gains?
<--- Score

53. What types of documentation is developed to ensure the application of data content and data value standards by staff members?
<--- Score

54. What other systems, operations, processes, and infrastructures (hiring practices, staffing, training, incentives/rewards, metrics/dashboards/scorecards, etc.) need updates, additions, changes, or deletions

in order to facilitate knowledge transfer and improvements?

<--- Score

55. What are your concerns regarding how to scale Managed Security Services to your organization?

<--- Score

56. Does the response plan contain a definite closed loop continual improvement scheme (e.g., plan-do-check-act)?

<--- Score

57. What is the backup plan?

<--- Score

58. What can you learn from a theory of complexity?

<--- Score

59. What is the ease of use and how big is the learning curve to effectively automate?

<--- Score

60. Is a response plan in place for when the input, process, or output measures indicate an 'out-of-control' condition?

<--- Score

61. How will the process owner and team be able to hold the gains?

<--- Score

62. Does a troubleshooting guide exist or is it needed?

<--- Score

63. Does your technology scale?

<--- Score

64. How will the process owner verify improvement in present and future sigma levels, process capabilities?

<--- Score

65. What other areas of the group might benefit from the Automation team's improvements, knowledge, and learning?

<--- Score

66. Which technologies is your organization currently employing or planning to employ?

<--- Score

67. How do you ensure model monitoring gets the appropriate level of attention it needs?

<--- Score

68. What does a disaster recovery plan look like?

<--- Score

69. Have new or revised work instructions resulted?

<--- Score

70. What are the operations requirements for system management and monitoring of the production system?

<--- Score

71. To what extent have the programming staff used custom controls?

<--- Score

72. Is there a documented and implemented

monitoring plan?
<--- Score

73. How might the group capture best practices and lessons learned so as to leverage improvements?
<--- Score

74. Are operating procedures consistent?
<--- Score

75. Is there a transfer of ownership and knowledge to process owner and process team tasked with the responsibilities.
<--- Score

76. What is learned by employing the internally focused analysis techniques of Duration Analysis and Activity-Based Costing?
<--- Score

77. Who owns what AI software learns as it gets smarter?
<--- Score

78. What quality tools were useful in the control phase?
<--- Score

79. Is reporting being used or needed?
<--- Score

80. How important do you expect your workforce capabilities to be in supporting your organizations future growth plans?
<--- Score

81. Which factors should you raise well above the industrys standard?
<--- Score

82. Does job training on the documented procedures need to be part of the process team's education and training?
<--- Score

83. Are there plans (or considerations) to update the brand identity?
<--- Score

84. How are individual contributions and learning achievements in the RPA team project assessed?
<--- Score

85. Are current automation solutions lagging behind in technological advancement, or are there advantages and economies of scale in conventional technology that benefits current design?
<--- Score

86. Are suggested corrective/restorative actions indicated on the response plan for known causes to problems that might surface?
<--- Score

87. Are new process steps, standards, and documentation ingrained into normal operations?
<--- Score

88. Has sound policy been established to guide control implementation and management?
<--- Score

89. What specific cost control initiatives, if any, are you planning and undertaking in the next financial year?

<--- Score

90. Are there plans to leverage e-commerce opportunities via a mobile app?

<--- Score

Add up total points for this section:
_____ = Total points for this section

Divided by: _____ (number of statements answered) = _____ Average score for this section

Transfer your score to the Automation Index at the beginning of the Self-Assessment.

CRITERION #7: SUSTAIN:

INTENT: Retain the benefits.

In my belief, the answer to this question is clearly defined:

5 Strongly Agree

4 Agree

3 Neutral

2 Disagree

1 Strongly Disagree

1. What is the appropriate level of automation?
<--- Score

2. The impact on jobs: Automation and anxiety, will smarter machines cause mass unemployment?
<--- Score

3. If a principal objective or accomplishment of this automation is to make labor savings, how much could you hope to save?
<--- Score

4. If resources can be relieved of tasks through automation, where will freed-up time be spent?

<--- Score

5. What kind of tests does the tool support?

<--- Score

6. How much effort is involved?

<--- Score

7. Where do the techniques for applying ML to IoT and Automation differ?

<--- Score

8. Do the process automations need to be in a secure data center, public cloud or private cloud?

<--- Score

9. Of the business processes in your organization, which could benefit most from automation?

<--- Score

10. What are the document types and volumes considered for automation?

<--- Score

11. What are you looking for?

<--- Score

12. Where does rpa sit on the automation agenda?

<--- Score

13. Robotic, intelligent, smart automation what does it take and are you ready for the next level of i&o automation?

<--- Score

14. What types of services not performed by your organization are commonly requested?
<--- Score

15. How frequently do you use marketing automation dashboards to track key performance outcomes?
<--- Score

16. In what order should the major software functions be incorporated?
<--- Score

17. Which is not an interface level that you could use automation for testing?
<--- Score

18. Does the expectation on automated GUI testing differ after the tests?
<--- Score

19. Can you enumerate all the interfaces in your software?
<--- Score

20. Application life-cycle: will the application be in production for months or years?
<--- Score

21. What makes an application a candidate for automation?
<--- Score

22. How do you induce random delays in your

automated GUI tests?

<--- Score

23. What feature/capability is most deficient in your current marketing automation platform?

<--- Score

24. Gdpr compliance - how does automation save the day for your organization?

<--- Score

25. What are the control system design challenges for more advanced forms of vehicle automation?

<--- Score

26. What are the requirements of the Marketing Automation system for your organization?

<--- Score

27. Does robotic process automation really help it achieve your business imperative of better, faster, for less?

<--- Score

28. Over what time period do you expect to see significant return on investment from a digital transformation, b artificial intelligence, and c robotic process automation?

<--- Score

29. If a gui has high value metrics, does that correctly indicate that it is more likely that this gui is less testable?

<--- Score

30. Is automation used to achieve consistency in

serving customers?

<--- Score

31. What are the distinctions between Email Marketing and Market Automation?

<--- Score

32. What are the changes that are necessary to implement automation?

<--- Score

33. Is automation technically feasible?

<--- Score

34. Where are the building automation control centers and cabinets located?

<--- Score

35. What are the options for training and support?

<--- Score

36. Can system effectiveness be improved by automation?

<--- Score

37. Can your organization benefit from more automation?

<--- Score

38. Is there a (electronic) records management policy?

<--- Score

39. How do you order Intelligent Automation Services?

<--- Score

40. Which generation is most at risk of job automation?

<--- Score

41. How do you design new processes for automation and how are you testing the automated jobs?

<--- Score

42. How do you feel about impact of automation/ robotics on your job?

<--- Score

43. When the engineering team is satisfied, and pushes the new features to a full automation run, including load testing, how long does it take to declare the service ready to use?

<--- Score

44. What automation tools are available for your Kanban board?

<--- Score

45. How are you defining success for each campaign?

<--- Score

46. Why do most Robotic Process Automation (Robotic Process Automation) projects experience difficulties when trying to move beyond the Proof of Concept or Pilot phase?

<--- Score

47. Do you use marketing automation?

<--- Score

48. Which transactions are best suited for Robotic Process Automation?

<--- Score

49. How will you keep your delivery continuous?

<--- Score

50. To what extent is Visual GUI Testing feasible for long-term use in industrial practice?

<--- Score

51. What can automated GUI testing not do that humans can?

<--- Score

52. Is there enough automation of controls and ongoing controls monitoring?

<--- Score

53. How important is it to scale the automations to more effectively manage the volumes of work?

<--- Score

54. How do you do glass box testing?

<--- Score

55. Unemployment has been low, even as the automation market has grown. Could the fears of robots stealing jobs be overblown?

<--- Score

56. How is robotic and cognitive automation transforming your industry?

<--- Score

57. How do you keep track of unexpected UI bugs during GUI Automation Load Tests?
<--- Score

58. Can the source code for any or all the applications be obtained in a short time frame, so that the details can be assessed and used to help guide you?
<--- Score

59. How will you ensure that the automation is executed using the latest version of the configuration?
<--- Score

60. Why should you use Robotic Process Automation?
<--- Score

61. Are the types of tests modular and capable of being shared across application domains?
<--- Score

62. What level of automation currently exists?
<--- Score

63. Is it critical to have a centralized enterprise view of the automations being executed, what is outstanding and which items require attention?
<--- Score

64. How can you prove that the IT system is good enough?
<--- Score

65. In what programming languages it is possible

to create tests?

<--- Score

66. When anomalies are found in testing, are they recorded?

<--- Score

67. What features do users use the most?

<--- Score

68. Does your organization have resources available to produce a report in formats?

<--- Score

69. Does the system respond in a timely manner?

<--- Score

70. How are you building workflows in the process automation design tool and are you using recorder versus design-based?

<--- Score

71. What environmental considerations must be taken into account when planning for automation?

<--- Score

72. What are the skills of your current staff?

<--- Score

73. Which factors did you create that the industry has never offered?

<--- Score

74. What is test automation?

<--- Score

75. Does the marketing automation system have the ability to create tasks for sales?

<--- Score

76. Could use of Robotic Process Automation and IA impair the IP indemnities under your licenses?

<--- Score

77. Is the behavior of the software under test the same with automation as without?

<--- Score

78. How do you establish a proper basis for initiating tasks for the next software life cycle activity?

<--- Score

79. In which functions do you use Robotic Process Automation?

<--- Score

80. Has your organization implemented a procedure for effective hand-off communication?

<--- Score

81. What tools can be used to capitalize on marketing automation?

<--- Score

82. What is available off-the-shelf that meets your demands for automation?

<--- Score

83. What growth or changes do you see in your document automation needs?

<--- Score

84. What new capabilities will Robotic Process Automation and AI enable?

<--- Score

85. How long does it take for a routine landing page update without a marketing automation system?

<--- Score

86. How do testers test the correctness of GUI interactions?

<--- Score

87. Is an agile automation / information system enough for the business to achieve agile production?

<--- Score

88. What is the end goal?

<--- Score

89. Do you use workload automation for big data automation?

<--- Score

90. How do you make sure that new versions of the services work with each other?

<--- Score

91. Are product sales meeting expectations?

<--- Score

92. Who is responsible for the management and support of corresponding systems?

<--- Score

93. To what degree will you be able to track usage to assess any benefits of document automation?
<--- Score

94. Have you identified areas in your business where automation is most relevant?
<--- Score

95. How is the ease of use of the tool?
<--- Score

96. Is there a program to reduce the volume of hazardous waste that is generated by your organization?
<--- Score

97. How will internal audit and compliance interact with the center of excellence (CoE)?
<--- Score

98. What is the return on investment for the tools?
<--- Score

99. Do you rely on third parties to manage intelligent automation processes or build your own CoE?
<--- Score

100. Is the website written in such a way that it can be accessed through an Automation API?
<--- Score

101. How does web tracking work?
<--- Score

102. What is the role of automation in the context of risk management?

<--- Score

103. Is there a current need to implement an automation tool for the PMO and if so what are the needs?

<--- Score

104. Are there specific aspects of automation that should be sought out when looking at Agile ALM tools?

<--- Score

105. Which processes are good candidates for automation?

<--- Score

106. How does your organization respond to a competitors price cut?

<--- Score

107. As systems and business requirements change, how important is ease of making changes to the automations?

<--- Score

108. What are the advantages of marketing automation?

<--- Score

109. Do you have tool success (or failure) stories to share?

<--- Score

110. To what degree have you implemented types

of automation in a production environment?

<--- Score

111. Does the solution provide sufficient process automation capabilities?

<--- Score

112. What problems can be improved with automation?

<--- Score

113. What do you mean by Enterprise Marketing Automation?

<--- Score

114. How do you partner with large corporations?

<--- Score

115. Which process criteria are best suited to Robotic Process Automation?

<--- Score

116. Does your organization have adequate resources to operationalize the system?

<--- Score

117. Does your testing community agree that they are adequately prepared for the Acceptance activities?

<--- Score

118. Do you have a cyber security concept tailored to your automation environment?

<--- Score

119. How can automation be viewed as

augmenting human potential rather than
displacing it?

<--- Score

120. What is essential to test automation design in
your organization?

<--- Score

121. What software life cycle do you use?

<--- Score

122. What is your current financial years Robotic
Process Automation budget for software and
services?

<--- Score

123. What level of process automation connects
your IT asset and service management processes?

<--- Score

124. What will be the next automation
improvements that will optimize the production
rates?

<--- Score

125. What about the nature of industrial data
streams and the legacy automation equipment
that is already out there?

<--- Score

126. Business is moving faster to the cloud,
and DevOps is accelerating scale and pushing
automation. How do you secure DevOps and cloud
deployments?

<--- Score

127. The lack of tools raises the question, what tools can be built, and shared for automation of darknet intelligence tradecraft?

<--- Score

128. Can print and mail be part of the marketing automation process?

<--- Score

129. Do you have a Marketing Automation system that you use in conjunction with Microsoft D365?

<--- Score

130. How can you predict that automation will yield beneficial outcome for your organization?

<--- Score

131. How do you select the right candidate for robotic process automation?

<--- Score

132. What is the purpose of the test execution report?

<--- Score

133. Does your system provide deliverability services?

<--- Score

134. Is it possible to create your own plug-ins and extensions to expand the tools functionality?

<--- Score

135. What is a limitation of test automation?

<--- Score

136. Is there automation and management tools?
<--- Score

137. Do you have Security Automation issues?
<--- Score

138. If you are doing custom programming, is there a contract that specifies the acceptance tests?
<--- Score

139. How efficient is the implementation when it comes to execution time?
<--- Score

140. How often is the system updated?
<--- Score

141. Who should conduct a post-implementation review?
<--- Score

142. Is the marketing automation system being used to its full potential?
<--- Score

143. Can the system run batch de-duplication?
<--- Score

144. What can you gain by using automated software testing tools?
<--- Score

145. Do you have the personnel to support document automation?
<--- Score

146. What is the strategy for re-deploying existing resources after automation?

<--- Score

147. Does your organization have a policy that addresses compliance with the CAP terms of accreditation?

<--- Score

148. Does the application have role-based access for customers and third party users?

<--- Score

149. Operability: are the features of the tool cumbersome to use, or prone to user error?

<--- Score

150. Desktop or server: which should be the focus of automation?

<--- Score

151. Are you seeing any patterns?

<--- Score

152. How do you attack test automation in a truly agile environment?

<--- Score

153. Wat is your organizations foremost challenge around realizing it operations management automation?

<--- Score

154. What financial considerations must be taken into account when planning an automation

project?
<--- Score

155. If you have used a keyword-driven approach to the test automation scripting and you now need to test new features that have been added, what do you do?
<--- Score

156. How does your organization currently use robotics and automation systems?
<--- Score

157. How do you provide guidance to contractors?
<--- Score

158. What metrics are you tracking to show the value of the test automation for this project?
<--- Score

159. Does your organization have a Quality Manager?
<--- Score

160. Can automated gui testing work with the kind of software you test?
<--- Score

161. What are the benefits of automation testing?
<--- Score

162. What one factor limits the adoption of more automation in your organization the most?
<--- Score

163. How important are the topics of diagnostics

and condition monitoring, especially from the point of view of One Cable Automation?

<--- Score

164. Does automation, electrification and the usage of algorithms change the goods and products that are traded?

<--- Score

165. Can each function be automated?

<--- Score

166. What are the resulting implications for Robotic Process Automation governance, skills sets and organization?

<--- Score

167. What concerns do you have about Robotic Process Automation?

<--- Score

168. Smart contracts: the ultimate automation of trust?

<--- Score

169. What effect will Robotic Process Automation and AI have on labor requirements?

<--- Score

170. How (and why) are you using marketing automation now?

<--- Score

171. Where are you in your current (system-level) test automation?

<--- Score

172. Do you typically experience a summer slowdown or speed up?

<--- Score

173. From the IT angle: what do you have to put in place in terms of an operating model and functionality to evolve and support an Enterprise deployment of robotic process automation?

<--- Score

174. Validation: are you building the right product?

<--- Score

175. How does the system operate during test?

<--- Score

176. Is further automation the way forward for augmenting human thinking and problem-solving?

<--- Score

177. Is there a procedure for the support of the computer system?

<--- Score

178. When should gui testing be conducted?

<--- Score

179. What roles and personnel are able to deliver all details, even when moving down the pyramid levels, for business process automation?

<--- Score

180. Where will automation fit into your business?

<--- Score

181. Who should perform a post-implementation review?
<--- Score

182. Which tools are involved in the automation of regression testing?
<--- Score

183. Process automation and tool integration: How well do the tools support lifecycle processes and what kind of tool integrations are there?
<--- Score

184. Do you do regression testing?
<--- Score

185. How can the cio drive robotic process automation as a strategic imperative?
<--- Score

186. What does the future hold as Robotic Process Automation becomes more and more prevalent in the business world?
<--- Score

187. Are the processes low-importance tactical automations based on localized practices and imperatives or are they high-value with high transaction volume?
<--- Score

188. Is there a history of Verification, Validation, and Accreditation in your organization?
<--- Score

189. What does a virtualized control system look like compared to a classic physical automation system?

<--- Score

190. How do you track progress of test automation?

<--- Score

191. What role does the C-suite play in capitalizing on AI, robotics, and automation?

<--- Score

192. Is the automation of this process required in a new information system?

<--- Score

193. What is the value of adding additional intelligence via programming to an automated script?

<--- Score

194. What do you lose with automation?

<--- Score

195. What are the main benefits of marketing automation for your organization?

<--- Score

196. How do you get workload information?

<--- Score

197. How much will automation play a role in helping your organization discover new drugs faster or process more patents?

<--- Score

198. When is the best time, for test automation, to consider legal and/or standards requirements?
<--- Score

199. Who in your organization should be involved in the adoption of Robotic Process Automation?
<--- Score

200. How do you validate and manage your corporate knowledge in IT Risk Management Automation: a patchwork process - or defend it to regulators?
<--- Score

201. What operating systems are supported?
<--- Score

202. The first step of marketing automation readiness is strategic alignment between sales and marketing: what are the primary objectives of your sales organization?
<--- Score

203. What type of management information system does your organization use?
<--- Score

204. What is your service automation?
<--- Score

205. What processes/departments are best suited for automation?
<--- Score

206. Will you implement a Blockchain based protocol for lot?

<--- Score

207. What does your organization look like when it combines all of the automation elements you have considered?

<--- Score

208. Are you looking to automate light tasks in an agent-augmentation role or a wholesale automation of end-to-end business processes that free up the human operator for higher-value tasks?

<--- Score

209. What types of automation are ready for prime time and which modules are the best candidates?

<--- Score

210. Are automation false alarms worse than misses?

<--- Score

211. How do you construct a productive test model that is capable of detecting defects efficiently?

<--- Score

212. What are the advantages of marketing automation to your organization?

<--- Score

213. What benefits can new automation and data exchange bring to highly compliant traders?

<--- Score

214. Will savings from automation be clearly visible?

<--- Score

215. Does the system de-duplicate leads from forms?

<--- Score

216. Can network evolution augment devops automation?

<--- Score

217. Does automation reduce time to results and increase quality management?

<--- Score

218. Are there automation and management tools?

<--- Score

219. How do you describe run rates and pass rates with models?

<--- Score

220. What scripting technique is used to build upon the structured scripting that has already been done and to implement this test automation to meet the business goals?

<--- Score

221. What is the level of automation that you can achieve?

<--- Score

222. Can the team be reasonably expected to efficiently use the tool?

<--- Score

223. Is a full-organization automation system appropriate for all types of laboratories?
<--- Score

224. Why Automate?
<--- Score

225. How much it involvement will robotic process automation implementation require?
<--- Score

226. What processes are suitable to deploy with Robotic Process Automation?
<--- Score

227. How does your organization know its spending the right amount?
<--- Score

228. How is it implemented to greatest effect?
<--- Score

229. Where do you go for automation products?
<--- Score

230. What are the post-automation goals for this process?
<--- Score

231. Robotic process automation buying decisions: who is influencing?
<--- Score

232. How much time and effort will it take to

implement Robotic Process Automation?
<--- Score

233. Whether initiated by business operations or IT executives, in all cases Robotic Process Automation plays straight into ITs better, faster for less dilemma. And with what results?
<--- Score

234. What do you test automate?
<--- Score

235. What materials do you use to perform calibration verification?
<--- Score

236. What sources of variability are critical?
<--- Score

237. Do you anticipate that the product will be translated to other languages?
<--- Score

238. Do you currently use a CRM or marketing automation platform?
<--- Score

239. How do you automatically relevant information from the test automation software?
<--- Score

240. How are ai/ml and automation coming together where, how, and why?
<--- Score

241. Who benefits from service automation?

<--- Score

242. Who in your organization will use the marketing automation system?
<--- Score

243. Which type of automation do you feel is most essential?
<--- Score

244. Do you have automation or deployment tools?
<--- Score

245. How do you know how good your code is?
<--- Score

246. How does automation fit into Quality Assurance?
<--- Score

247. How does your organization deliver a best-in-class customer experience that meets or exceeds the expectations set by customers?
<--- Score

248. What can automated GUI testing do that a human can not do?
<--- Score

249. How does robotic process automation fit in your team/organization?
<--- Score

250. Why do you need automation?
<--- Score

251. Do you need a marketing automation system?
<--- Score

252. Can you track and reserve compliance in any automation chain or even step?
<--- Score

253. Does your organization have a policy to protect personnel from excessive noise levels?
<--- Score

254. To what extent will process automation replace traditional, human workers in your organization?
<--- Score

255. What is the power of an automation policy?
<--- Score

256. Who should receive a post-implementation review report?
<--- Score

257. Do you have a high level of process automation connecting your IT asset and service management?
<--- Score

258. Robotic, intelligent, smart automation - what does it take and is your organization ready for the next level of i&o automation?
<--- Score

259. Who are the current internal and external users of robotics and automation?

<--- Score

260. On which operating system is a given GUI application more performant?
<--- Score

261. What is essential to test automation design?
<--- Score

262. What are the biggest hurdles to overcome when deciding whether or not to go for automation of PV?
<--- Score

263. Do you already have documents that can form the basis of document automation tools?
<--- Score

264. Do you estimate the benefits of automation on a process-by-process basis, so that if resources can be relieved of tasks through automation, where will freed-up time be spent?
<--- Score

265. If you are using marketing automation, how does this help to enhance the digital marketing actions and what processes are automated?
<--- Score

266. Workers are an often overlooked source of great automation ideas, are you asking What task do you least like doing?
<--- Score

267. What are key benefits of automation to be achieved?

<--- Score

268. Are you able to improve productivity through innovations such as RFID, voice, and automation technologies?

<--- Score

269. Does your system have support for HTML import?

<--- Score

270. How is automation of software testing done?

<--- Score

271. Is automation cost effective?

<--- Score

272. Is automated gui testing valid for your organization?

<--- Score

273. What robotic process automation solutions are there on the market?

<--- Score

274. Which of the factors that your industry takes for granted should you eliminate?

<--- Score

275. Gui tests are brittle, is there a way to make it less brittle through design?

<--- Score

276. Of the person who knows most about the test automation toolset: what is its track record at coping with product change?

<--- Score

277. Are security orchestration and automation tools making a dent in the productivity issue?
<--- Score

278. What business functions can benefit from Robotic Process Automation?
<--- Score

279. How has this change affected the profession?
<--- Score

280. Will robotic process automation herald a new digital era in regulatory compliance in banks?
<--- Score

281. How comfortable (and capable) is the team in regard to automation?
<--- Score

282. How and where will the software be tested?
<--- Score

283. What creates the difference between basic robotic process automation and enterprise robotic process automation?
<--- Score

284. Is any system too small for a post-implementation review?
<--- Score

285. How do you manage and prioritize the demand pipeline for automation?
<--- Score

286. Do you have sales force automation?
<--- Score

287. Do you have tests you run on every build?
<--- Score

288. To what extent do current processes need to be reengineered as part of automation?
<--- Score

289. What services does your organization provide that are contracted out to another entity?
<--- Score

290. How do you perform a post-implementation review?
<--- Score

291. Why virtualize an automation system?
<--- Score

292. Do you have an appropriate level of automation and systems to accurately and efficiently fulfill orders?
<--- Score

293. How do you do black box testing?
<--- Score

294. What does not make sense to automate?
<--- Score

295. How do virtual machine features affect the performance of interactive applications?
<--- Score

296. In what ways has automation impacted your organization?

<--- Score

297. If a step fails, how would you know?

<--- Score

298. How do you synch infrastructure with virtualization automation?

<--- Score

299. How can AIOps and machine learning help increase automation across your toolchain?

<--- Score

300. What can robotic process automation do for your organization?

<--- Score

301. Are scripts for Robotic Process Automation software useful without the base software?

<--- Score

302. Why is automation necessary?

<--- Score

303. When your automation reports that a test passed, did it really?

<--- Score

304. In considering automation in your IT organization, what should be done first?

<--- Score

305. How is the evolution of the marketing

automation market: Where it is going, which niches?

<--- Score

306. Does it have an office automation system?

<--- Score

307. When does automation of GUI testing pay off?

<--- Score

308. What automation capabilities do you offer?

<--- Score

309. Are automations affected by using enhanced segmentation?

<--- Score

310. What is the percentage of repeat testing?

<--- Score

311. How do you provide training for contractors?

<--- Score

312. What are the best use cases for Robotic Process Automation?

<--- Score

313. What will an agile information system and automation system look like?

<--- Score

314. Is the effectiveness of the considered technique influenced by a parallel implementation?

<--- Score

315. Where will you gain the most advantages from automation, and where do your biggest inefficiencies lie?

<--- Score

316. Is the Product configured with access for and the parts shaped for the implementation of automation?

<--- Score

317. Does the system de-duplicate leads on import?

<--- Score

318. How will xml impact industrial automation?

<--- Score

319. How much has automating your applications increased your research productivity?

<--- Score

320. Is the social web being irreversibly corrupted by automation tools?

<--- Score

321. Where should you be careful?

<--- Score

322. How does automation affect the product/ service design specifications and procedures?

<--- Score

323. How do you ensure reliability of software?

<--- Score

324. Do you use automation to conduct third-

party due diligence?
<--- Score

325. Reliability and high quality are essential characteristics of any solution used in industrial substation automation. Which products on the market live up to their claims of meeting the most stringent standards in quality?
<--- Score

326. What kind of marketing automation platform do you need?
<--- Score

327. How do you know whether to use business process automation, business process improvement, or business process reengineering?
<--- Score

328. Where are you seeing the most use of automation?
<--- Score

329. What operational changes, if any have you implemented to meet increasing demands/ reduced resources?
<--- Score

330. Will the use of automation for testing render manual testers obsolete?
<--- Score

331. What is the level of process automation for contract management?
<--- Score

332. How much time is saved by automating this?
<--- Score

333. Which function is primarily responsible for funding Robotic Process Automation software and services?
<--- Score

334. Verification: are you building the product right?
<--- Score

335. How do you avoid breaking the tests when making the next iteration?
<--- Score

336. How stable is the behavior of the code under test?
<--- Score

337. Have product sales met expectations?
<--- Score

338. Is automation in place to do the deploy?
<--- Score

339. How will it roles be impacted by automation and ai in five years time?
<--- Score

340. Do current systems provide the required high levels of automation across the full process spectrum?
<--- Score

341. What are the types of tests that can be

automated?

<--- Score

342. Does your organization have procedures to ensure compliance with HIPAA?

<--- Score

343. Which areas of service management can benefit from automation?

<--- Score

344. What do you get for the price you are paying?

<--- Score

345. Does the increasing automation and utilization of algorithms produce more rational, better assessable and more predictable financial markets?

<--- Score

346. What will your organization of the future look like?

<--- Score

347. What level of control / automation is needed?

<--- Score

348. What do companies, that already use marketing automation, have to say?

<--- Score

349. Final point to consider before you start comparing vendors: What other tools will your marketing automation system need to integrate with?

<--- Score

350. What does it mean to have a million hits a day ?

<--- Score

351. Does the organization allow someone other than personnel to stock a machine, with safeguards of automation considered?

<--- Score

352. Are there any other key benefits to automation that you see?

<--- Score

353. People. Dont overlook the importance of people in keeping all the automation running smoothly. Are certain systems or applications dependent on one employee?

<--- Score

354. Visual gui testing in continuous integration; how beneficial is it and what are the drawbacks?

<--- Score

355. What domains are notably absent from contemporary inquiryies on algorithms, automation, and politics?

<--- Score

356. What makes a great automation candidate?

<--- Score

357. How flexible can each testing organization be regarding the final automation solution?

<--- Score

Add up total points for this section:
_____ = Total points for this section

Divided by: _____ (number of
statements answered) = _____
Average score for this section

Transfer your score to the Automation
Index at the beginning of the Self-
Assessment.

Automation and Managing Projects, Criteria for Project Managers:

1.0 Initiating Process Group: Automation

1. How well did the chosen processes produce the expected results?

2. Establishment of pm office?

3. How do you help others satisfy needs?

4. Realistic - are the desired results expressed in a way that the team will be motivated and believe that the required level of involvement will be obtained?

5. The process to Manage Stakeholders is part of which process group?

6. Are you just doing busywork to pass the time?

7. Are stakeholders properly informed about the status of the Automation project?

8. How well did you do?

9. Professionals want to know what is expected from them what are the deliverables?

10. Contingency planning. if a risk event occurs, what will you do?

11. Measurable - are the targets measurable?

12. During which stage of Risk planning are modeling techniques used to determine overall effects of risks on Automation project objectives for high probability,

high impact risks?

13. What are the short and long term implications?

14. Were escalated issues resolved promptly?

15. Have the stakeholders identified all individual requirements pertaining to business process?

16. Do you understand the quality and control criteria that must be achieved for successful Automation project completion?

17. How will you do it?

18. Do you know the roles & responsibilities required for this Automation project?

19. Does the Automation project team have enough people to execute the Automation project plan?

20. Are you properly tracking the progress of the Automation project and communicating the status to stakeholders?

1.1 Project Charter: Automation

21. Avoid costs, improve service, and/ or comply with a mandate?

22. What are you striving to accomplish (measurable goal(s))?

23. What are you trying to accomplish?

24. How high should you set your goals?

25. Did your Automation project ask for this?

26. How do you manage integration?

27. Automation project background: what is the primary motivation for this Automation project?

28. Does the Automation project need to consider any special capacity or capability issues?

29. When?

30. Are you building in-house ?

31. Pop quiz – which are the same inputs as in the Automation project charter?

32. Who will take notes, document decisions?

33. How are Automation projects different from operations?

34. What changes can you make to improve?

35. Is time of the essence?

36. Customer: who are you doing the Automation project for?

37. Review the general mission What system will be affected by the improvement efforts?

38. Assumptions and constraints: what assumptions were made in defining the Automation project?

39. Must Have?

40. Why is it important?

1.2 Stakeholder Register: Automation

41. Who are the stakeholders?

42. How will reports be created?

43. Is your organization ready for change?

44. Who wants to talk about Security?

45. What & Why?

46. Who is managing stakeholder engagement?

47. What is the power of the stakeholder?

48. How should employers make voices heard?

49. What opportunities exist to provide communications?

50. How big is the gap?

51. How much influence do they have on the Automation project?

52. What are the major Automation project milestones requiring communications or providing communications opportunities?

1.3 Stakeholder Analysis Matrix: Automation

53. Is changing technology threatening your organizations position?

54. Are there people who ise voices or interests in the issue may not be heard?

55. How do they affect the Automation project and its outcomes?

56. What mechanisms are proposed to monitor and measure Automation project performance in terms of social development outcomes?

57. Seasonality, weather effects?

58. Does your organization have bad debt or cash-flow problems?

59. Resources, assets, people?

60. How are you predicting what future (work)loads will be?

61. Who is directly responsible for decisions on issues important to the Automation project?

62. Identify the stakeholders levels most frequently used –or at least sought– in your Automation projects and for which purpose?

63. Innovative aspects?

64. How to measure the achievement of the Immediate Objective?

65. How to measure the achievement of the Outputs?

66. How will the stakeholder directly benefit from the Automation project and how will this affect the stakeholders motivation?

67. What tools would help you communicate?

68. Which resources are required?

69. Who will promote/support the Automation project, provided that they are involved?

70. Management cover, succession?

71. Are you going to weigh the stakeholders?

72. Partnership opportunities/synergies?

2.0 Planning Process Group: Automation

73. Why do it Automation projects fail?

74. To what extent do the intervention objectives and strategies of the Automation project respond to your organizations plans?

75. Does the program have follow-up mechanisms (to verify the quality of the products, punctuality of delivery, etc.) to measure progress in the achievement of the envisaged results?

76. What will you do to minimize the impact should a risk event occur?

77. When developing the estimates for Automation project phases, you choose to add the individual estimates for the activities that comprise each phase. What type of estimation method are you using?

78. Professionals want to know what is expected from them; what are the deliverables?

79. First of all, should any action be taken?

80. If task x starts two days late, what is the effect on the Automation project end date?

81. What makes your Automation project successful?

82. What is the NEXT thing to do?

83. What good practices or successful experiences or transferable examples have been identified?

84. If a risk event occurs, what will you do?

85. Explanation: is what the Automation project intents to solve a hard question?

86. Is your organization showing technical capacity and leadership commitment to keep working with the Automation project and to repeat it?

87. Have operating capacities been created and/or reinforced in partners?

88. What is the difference between the early schedule and late schedule?

89. What input will you be required to provide the Automation project team?

90. Is the Automation project making progress in helping to achieve the set results?

91. Why is it important to determine activity sequencing on Automation projects?

92. What is a Software Development Life Cycle (SDLC)?

2.1 Project Management Plan: Automation

93. Is there anything you would now do differently on your Automation project based on past experience?

94. Why do you manage integration?

95. What if, for example, the positive direction and vision of your organization causes expected trends to change resulting in greater need than expected?

96. Do the proposed changes from the Automation project include any significant risks to safety?

97. Are alternatives safe, functional, constructible, economical, reasonable and sustainable?

98. Is mitigation authorized or recommended?

99. Is the appropriate plan selected based on your organizations objectives and evaluation criteria expressed in Principles and Guidelines policies?

100. What goes into your Automation project Charter?

101. Are there any scope changes proposed for a previously authorized Automation project?

102. What are the deliverables?

103. Who is the sponsor?

104. What is Automation project scope management?

105. What should you drop in order to add something new?

106. Are there non-structural buyout or relocation recommendations?

107. What data/reports/tools/etc. do your PMs need?

108. What worked well?

109. Are there any client staffing expectations?

110. What are the constraints?

111. Who manages integration?

2.2 Scope Management Plan: Automation

112. Have adequate procedures been put in place for Automation project communication and status reporting across Automation project boundaries (for example interdependent software development among interfacing systems)?

113. Is the assigned Automation project manager a PMP (Certified Automation project manager) and experienced?

114. Timeline and milestones?

115. Are internal Automation project status meetings held at reasonable intervals?

116. Are Automation project team members involved in detailed estimating and scheduling?

117. Do you have funding for Automation project and product development, implementation and on-going support?

118. Is a pmo (Automation project management office) in place and provide oversight to the Automation project?

119. Does the title convey to the reader the essence of the Automation project?

120. Are decisions captured in a decisions log?

121. Do you have the reasons why the changes to your organizational systems and capabilities are required?

122. Has a capability assessment been conducted?

123. Materials available for performing the work?

124. How do you know how you are doing?

125. Will anyone else be involved in verifying the deliverables?

126. Are the budget estimates reasonable?

127. Are schedule deliverables actually delivered?

128. Is an industry recognized mechanized support tool(s) being used for Automation project scheduling & tracking?

129. Process groups – where do scope management processes fit in?

130. Do all stakeholders know how to access this repository and where to find the Automation project documentation?

2.3 Requirements Management Plan: Automation

131. Will the product release be stable and mature enough to be deployed in the user community?

132. Do you expect stakeholders to be cooperative?

133. Controlling Automation project requirements involves monitoring the status of the Automation project requirements and managing changes to the requirements. Who is responsible for monitoring and tracking the Automation project requirements?

134. How will bidders price evaluations be done, by deliverables, phases, or in a big bang?

135. Do you have an agreed upon process for alerting the Automation project Manager if a request for change in requirements leads to a product scope change?

136. Has the requirements team been instructed in the Change Control process?

137. What performance metrics will be used?

138. How do you know that you have done this right?

139. How will you develop the schedule of requirements activities?

140. Will you use an assessment of the Automation

project environment as a tool to discover risk to the requirements process?

141. How detailed should the Automation project get?

142. In case of software development; Should you have a test for each code module?

143. Subject to change control?

144. Describe the process for rejecting the Automation project requirements. Who has the authority to reject Automation project requirements?

145. Did you use declarative statements?

146. Who came up with this requirement?

147. Do you have an appropriate arrangement for meetings?

148. Is any organizational data being used or stored?

149. Could inaccurate or incomplete requirements in this Automation project create a serious risk for the business?

150. Should you include sub-activities?

2.4 Requirements Documentation: Automation

151. What marketing channels do you want to use: e-mail, letter or sms?

152. What happens when requirements are wrong?

153. How can you document system requirements?

154. What is a show stopper in the requirements?

155. Have the benefits identified with the system being identified clearly?

156. What is the risk associated with cost and schedule?

157. Is the requirement realistically testable?

158. Where do system and software requirements come from, what are sources?

159. How much does requirements engineering cost?

160. What are the attributes of a customer?

161. Is the origin of the requirement clearly stated?

162. Can you check system requirements?

163. How will requirements be documented and who signs off on them?

164. What will be the integration problems?

165. How to document system requirements?

166. What are the acceptance criteria?

167. Do your constraints stand?

168. Consistency. are there any requirements conflicts?

169. Where are business rules being captured?

170. Where do you define what is a customer, what are the attributes of customer?

2.5 Requirements Traceability Matrix: Automation

171. Why use a WBS?

172. What is the WBS?

173. What percentage of Automation projects are producing traceability matrices between requirements and other work products?

174. Describe the process for approving requirements so they can be added to the traceability matrix and Automation project work can be performed. Will the Automation project requirements become approved in writing?

175. How small is small enough?

176. How will it affect the stakeholders personally in their career?

177. Will you use a Requirements Traceability Matrix?

178. Why do you manage scope?

179. How do you manage scope?

180. Do you have a clear understanding of all subcontracts in place?

181. What are the chronologies, contingencies, consequences, criteria?

182. Is there a requirements traceability process in place?

2.6 Project Scope Statement: Automation

183. Any new risks introduced or old risks impacted. Are there issues that could affect the existing requirements for the result, service, or product if the scope changes?

184. Write a brief purpose statement for this Automation project. Include a business justification statement. What is the product of this Automation project?

185. Were potential customers involved early in the planning process?

186. Is there a Quality Assurance Plan documented and filed?

187. Will the risk documents be filed?

188. What is the product of this Automation project?

189. Have you been able to thoroughly document the Automation projects assumptions and constraints?

190. Will the Automation project risks be managed according to the Automation projects risk management process?

191. Why do you need to manage scope?

192. Are there issues that could affect the existing

requirements for the result, service, or product if the scope changes?

193. What are the defined meeting materials?

194. Will an issue form be in use?

195. Are there adequate Automation project control systems?

196. Is the Automation project manager qualified and experienced in Automation project management?

197. Where and how does the team fit within your organization structure?

198. Elements that deal with providing the detail?

199. Will the risk plan be updated on a regular and frequent basis?

200. Is the plan for your organization of the Automation project resources adequate?

201. If the scope changes, what will the impact be to your Automation project in terms of duration, cost, quality, or any other important areas of the Automation project?

202. If you were to write a list of what should not be included in the scope statement, what are the things that you would recommend be described as out-of-scope?

2.7 Assumption and Constraint Log: Automation

203. Are there processes defining how software will be developed including development methods, overall timeline for development, software product standards, and traceability?

204. Is the current scope of the Automation project substantially different than that originally defined in the approved Automation project plan?

205. What does an audit system look like?

206. Are formal code reviews conducted?

207. What threats might prevent you from getting there?

208. Have all necessary approvals been obtained?

209. Were the system requirements formally reviewed prior to initiating the design phase?

210. Is there adequate stakeholder participation for the vetting of requirements definition, changes and management?

211. Security analysis has access to information that is sanitized?

212. Can you perform this task or activity in a more effective manner?

213. If appropriate, is the deliverable content consistent with current Automation project documents and in compliance with the Document Management Plan?

214. Was the document/deliverable developed per the appropriate or required standards (for example, Institute of Electrical and Electronics Engineers standards)?

215. Violation trace: why ?

216. What do you audit?

217. Are there cosmetic errors that hinder readability and comprehension?

218. No superfluous information or marketing narrative?

219. Does the system design reflect the requirements?

220. Are processes for release management of new development from coding and unit testing, to integration testing, to training, and production defined and followed?

221. Has a Automation project Communications Plan been developed?

2.8 Work Breakdown Structure: Automation

222. How big is a work-package?

223. When would you develop a Work Breakdown Structure?

224. Is it a change in scope?

225. Is the work breakdown structure (wbs) defined and is the scope of the Automation project clear with assigned deliverable owners?

226. What has to be done?

227. When does it have to be done?

228. How far down?

229. Is it still viable?

230. How will you and your Automation project team define the Automation projects scope and work breakdown structure?

231. What is the probability that the Automation project duration will exceed xx weeks?

232. Who has to do it?

233. Where does it take place?

234. Why would you develop a Work Breakdown Structure?

235. Do you need another level?

236. Why is it useful?

237. When do you stop?

238. How much detail?

239. How many levels?

240. Can you make it?

241. What is the probability of completing the Automation project in less that xx days?

2.9 WBS Dictionary: Automation

242. Identify and isolate causes of favorable and unfavorable cost and schedule variances?

243. Actual cost of work performed?

244. Does the contractors system provide for accurate cost accumulation and assignment to control accounts in a manner consistent with the budgets using recognized acceptable costing techniques?

245. Do work packages reflect the actual way in which the work will be done and are they meaningful products or management-oriented subdivisions of a higher level element of work?

246. Do work packages consist of discrete tasks which are adequately described?

247. Are data elements summarized through the functional organizational structure for progressively higher levels of management?

248. Software specification, development, integration, and testing, licenses ?

249. Is work progressively subdivided into detailed work packages as requirements are defined?

250. Are the overhead pools formally and adequately identified?

251. Are time-phased budgets established for

planning and control of level of effort activity by category of resource; for example, type of manpower and/or material?

252. Are data elements reconcilable between internal summary reports and reports forwarded to us?

253. Is cost performance measurement at the point in time most suitable for the category of material involved, and no earlier than the time of actual receipt of material?

254. Contractor financial periods; for example, annual?

255. Is the work done on a work package level as described in the WBS dictionary?

256. Is work properly classified as measured effort, LOE, or apportioned effort and appropriately separated?

257. Are current work performance indicators and goals relatable to original goals as modified by contractual changes, replanning, and reprogramming actions?

258. Are current budgets resulting from changes to the authorized work and/or internal replanning, reconcilable to original budgets for specified reporting items?

259. Are all elements of indirect expense identified to overhead cost budgets of Automation projections?

2.10 Schedule Management Plan: Automation

260. Are risk triggers captured?

261. Are metrics used to evaluate and manage Vendors?

262. Have key stakeholders been identified?

263. Does the ims include all contract and/or designated management control milestones?

264. Is a process for scheduling and reporting defined, including forms and formats?

265. Are the activity durations realistic and at an appropriate level of detail for effective management?

266. Are the results of quality assurance reviews provided to affected groups & individuals?

267. Are all vendor contracts closed out?

268. Is the quality assurance team identified?

269. Was the scope definition used in task sequencing?

270. Were the budget estimates reasonable?

271. Is documentation created for communication with the suppliers and Vendors?

272. Is the ims development and management approach described?

273. Are the schedule estimates reasonable given the Automation project?

274. Are action items captured and managed?

275. What happens if a warning is triggered?

276. Which status reports are received per the Automation project Plan?

277. Has a sponsor been identified?

278. Have the procedures for identifying budget variances been followed?

279. Have Automation project success criteria been defined?

2.11 Activity List: Automation

280. What are you counting on?

281. How much slack is available in the Automation project?

282. Can you determine the activity that must finish, before this activity can start?

283. What went right?

284. How should ongoing costs be monitored to try to keep the Automation project within budget?

285. What is the total time required to complete the Automation project if no delays occur?

286. In what sequence?

287. What did not go as well?

288. Is there anything planned that does not need to be here?

289. The wbs is developed as part of a joint planning session. and how do you know that youhave done this right?

290. What is your organizations history in doing similar activities?

291. Are the required resources available or need to be acquired?

292. Is infrastructure setup part of your Automation project?

293. What went well?

294. How detailed should a Automation project get?

295. How will it be performed?

296. How can the Automation project be displayed graphically to better visualize the activities?

297. How difficult will it be to do specific activities on this Automation project?

298. Who will perform the work?

2.12 Activity Attributes: Automation

299. What conclusions/generalizations can you draw from this?

300. Activity: fair or not fair?

301. How many days do you need to complete the work scope with a limit of X number of resources?

302. Does your organization of the data change its meaning?

303. Were there other ways you could have organized the data to achieve similar results?

304. How many resources do you need to complete the work scope within a limit of X number of days?

305. Can more resources be added?

306. Are the required resources available?

307. How difficult will it be to complete specific activities on this Automation project?

308. Why?

309. What is missing?

310. Has management defined a definite timeframe for the turnaround or Automation project window?

311. Would you consider either of corresponding

activities an outlier?

312. Activity: what is In the Bag?

313. Which method produces the more accurate cost assignment?

314. Is there a trend during the year?

315. Can you re-assign any activities to another resource to resolve an over-allocation?

2.13 Milestone List: Automation

316. Calculate how long can activity be delayed?

317. Timescales, deadlines and pressures?

318. Can you derive how soon can the whole Automation project finish?

319. Do you foresee any technical risks or developmental challenges?

320. How difficult will it be to do specific activities on this Automation project?

321. Own known vulnerabilities?

322. Who will manage the Automation project on a day-to-day basis?

323. Gaps in capabilities?

324. It is to be a narrative text providing the crucial aspects of your Automation project proposal answering what, who, how, when and where?

325. How late can the activity start?

326. Obstacles faced?

327. What specific improvements did you make to the Automation project proposal since the previous time?

328. Describe the industry you are in and the market

growth opportunities. What is the market for your technology, product or service?

329. Environmental effects?

330. Loss of key staff?

331. Describe the concept of the technology, product or service that will be or has been developed. How will it be used?

332. How will you get the word out to customers?

333. Insurmountable weaknesses?

334. Continuity, supply chain robustness?

2.14 Network Diagram: Automation

335. If the Automation project network diagram cannot change and you have extra personnel resources, what is the BEST thing to do?

336. Why must you schedule milestones, such as reviews, throughout the Automation project?

337. What to do and When?

338. Are you on time?

339. What is the completion time?

340. What activity must be completed immediately before this activity can start?

341. If x is long, what would be the completion time if you break x into two parallel parts of y weeks and z weeks?

342. Can you calculate the confidence level?

343. What activities must occur simultaneously with this activity?

344. What must be completed before an activity can be started?

345. Review the logical flow of the network diagram. Take a look at which activities you have first and then sequence the activities. Do they make sense?

346. Will crashing x weeks return more in benefits than it costs?

347. Which type of network diagram allows you to depict four types of dependencies?

348. What job or jobs could run concurrently?

349. What can be done concurrently?

350. How confident can you be in your milestone dates and the delivery date?

351. Where do schedules come from?

352. What is the lowest cost to complete this Automation project in xx weeks?

2.15 Activity Resource Requirements: Automation

353. Do you use tools like decomposition and rolling-wave planning to produce the activity list and other outputs?

354. How do you manage time?

355. Organizational Applicability?

356. Are there unresolved issues that need to be addressed?

357. How many signatures do you require on a check and does this match what is in your policy and procedures?

358. What is the Work Plan Standard?

359. Which logical relationship does the PDM use most often?

360. How do you handle petty cash?

361. What are constraints that you might find during the Human Resource Planning process?

362. Anything else?

363. Other support in specific areas?

364. Time for overtime?

365. When does monitoring begin?

366. Why do you do that?

2.16 Resource Breakdown Structure: Automation

367. How can this help you with team building?

368. What is the difference between % Complete and % work?

369. Who is allowed to see what data about which resources?

370. What is the primary purpose of the human resource plan?

371. Who will use the system?

372. When do they need the information?

373. How should the information be delivered?

374. Why is this important?

375. What is the purpose of assigning and documenting responsibility?

376. What went wrong?

377. What are the requirements for resource data?

378. Who needs what information?

379. What can you do to improve productivity?

380. Any changes from stakeholders?

2.17 Activity Duration Estimates: Automation

381. Given your research into similar classes and the work you think is required for this Automation project, what assumptions, variables, or costs would you change from the information provided above?

382. Is the work performed reviewed against contractual objectives?

383. Will the new application be developed using existing hardware, software, and networks?

384. Are contractor costs, schedule and technical performance monitored throughout the Automation project?

385. How is the Automation project doing?

386. What is pmp certification, and why do you think the number of people earning it has grown so much in the past ten years?

387. How do theories relate to Automation project management?

388. How does a Automation project life cycle differ from a product life cycle?

389. Are risks that are likely to affect the Automation project identified and documented?

390. How does Automation project integration management relate to the Automation project life cycle, stakeholders, and the other Automation project management knowledge areas?

391. What functions does this software provide that cannot be done easily using other tools such as a spreadsheet or database?

392. Which skills do you think are most important for an information technology Automation project manager?

393. Are updates on work results collected and used as inputs to the performance reporting process?

394. Are adjustments implemented to correct or prevent defects?

395. Which suggestions do you find most useful?

396. Will it help in finding or retaining employees?

397. Which includes asking team members about the time estimates for activities and reaching agreement on the calendar date for each activity?

398. Do an internet search on earning pmp certification. be sure to search for yahoo groups related to this topic. what are the options you found to help people prepare for the exam?

399. Who will provide training for the new application?

2.18 Duration Estimating Worksheet: Automation

400. Is this operation cost effective?

401. Science = process: remember the scientific method?

402. Small or large Automation project?

403. Can the Automation project be constructed as planned?

404. When do the individual activities need to start and finish?

405. For other activities, how much delay can be tolerated?

406. What are the critical bottleneck activities?

407. What is cost and Automation project cost management?

408. Why estimate costs?

409. How should ongoing costs be monitored to try to keep the Automation project within budget?

410. When, then?

411. What info is needed?

412. Done before proceeding with this activity or what can be done concurrently?

413. Do any colleagues have experience with your organization and/or RFPs?

414. When does your organization expect to be able to complete it?

415. How can the Automation project be displayed graphically to better visualize the activities?

416. Why estimate time and cost?

417. What utility impacts are there?

2.19 Project Schedule: Automation

418. What is the difference?

419. What is risk management?

420. Understand the constraints used in preparing the schedule. Are activities connected because logic dictates the order in which others occur?

421. Is Automation project work proceeding in accordance with the original Automation project schedule?

422. What is risk?

423. Automation project work estimates Who is managing the work estimate quality of work tasks in the Automation project schedule?

424. Change management required?

425. Are the original Automation project schedule and budget realistic?

426. Is the Automation project schedule available for all Automation project team members to review?

427. Why do you need schedules?

428. Schedule/cost recovery?

429. Is there a Schedule Management Plan that establishes the criteria and activities for developing,

monitoring and controlling the Automation project schedule?

430. Is the structure for tracking the Automation project schedule well defined and assigned to a specific individual?

431. Are activities connected because logic dictates the order in which others occur?

432. Eliminate unnecessary activities. Are there activities that came from a template or previous Automation project that are not applicable on this phase of this Automation project?

433. How can you address that situation?

434. If you can not fix it, how do you do it differently?

2.20 Cost Management Plan: Automation

435. Has a quality assurance plan been developed for the Automation project?

436. Cost variances – how will cost variances be identified and corrected?

437. How relevant is this attribute to this Automation project or audit?

438. Does the Automation project have a Quality Culture?

439. Forecasts – how will the time and resources needed to complete the Automation project be forecast?

440. Have Automation project management standards and procedures been identified / established and documented?

441. Are non-critical path items updated and agreed upon with the teams?

442. Are the people assigned to the Automation project sufficiently qualified?

443. Responsibilities – what is the split of responsibilities between the owner and contractors?

444. Are vendor invoices audited for accuracy before

payment?

445. Are meeting minutes captured and sent out after the meeting?

446. Is your organization certified as a supplier, wholesaler and/or regular dealer?

447. Risk rating?

448. Are estimating assumptions and constraints captured?

449. Contingency – how will cost contingency be administered?

450. Cost tracking and performance analysis – How will cost tracking and performance analysis be accomplished?

451. Designated small business reserve?

452. Is an industry recognized mechanized support tool(s) being used for Automation project scheduling & tracking?

2.21 Activity Cost Estimates: Automation

453. How do you manage cost?

454. What is your organizations history in doing similar tasks?

455. Were you satisfied with the work?

456. How do you treat administrative costs in the activity inventory?

457. Does the activity serve a common type of customer?

458. How Award?

459. How difficult will it be to do specific tasks on the Automation project?

460. Does the activity rely on a common set of tools to carry it out?

461. What makes a good activity description?

462. Does the estimator have experience?

463. What happens if you cannot produce the documentation for the single audit?

464. What makes a good expected result statement?

465. Where can you get activity reports?

466. In which phase of the acquisition process cycle does source qualifications reside?

467. What areas does the group agree are the biggest success on the Automation project?

468. Will you use any tools, such as Automation project management software, to assist in capturing Earned Value metrics?

469. One way to define activities is to consider how organization employees describe jobs to families and friends. You basically want to know, What do you do?

470. Who & what determines the need for contracted services?

471. Can you delete activities or make them inactive?

472. Scope statement only direct or indirect costs as well?

2.22 Cost Estimating Worksheet: Automation

473. Who is best positioned to know and assist in identifying corresponding factors?

474. Ask: are others positioned to know, are others credible, and will others cooperate?

475. Can a trend be established from historical performance data on the selected measure and are the criteria for using trend analysis or forecasting methods met?

476. What costs are to be estimated?

477. Does the Automation project provide innovative ways for stakeholders to overcome obstacles or deliver better outcomes?

478. Is it feasible to establish a control group arrangement?

479. Is the Automation project responsive to community need?

480. Identify the timeframe necessary to monitor progress and collect data to determine how the selected measure has changed?

481. What can be included?

482. Will the Automation project collaborate with the

local community and leverage resources?

483. What additional Automation project(s) could be initiated as a result of this Automation project?

484. What happens to any remaining funds not used?

485. What is the estimated labor cost today based upon this information?

486. What will others want?

487. What is the purpose of estimating?

488. How will the results be shared and to whom?

489. Value pocket identification & quantification what are value pockets?

2.23 Cost Baseline: Automation

490. How accurate do cost estimates need to be?

491. Have all the product or service deliverables been accepted by the customer?

492. What deliverables come first?

493. Has training and knowledge transfer of the operations organization been completed?

494. Have the lessons learned been filed with the Automation project Management Office?

495. Definition of done can be traced back to the definitions of what are you providing to the customer in terms of deliverables?

496. Are you asking management for something as a result of this update?

497. What can go wrong?

498. Has the Automation project documentation been archived or otherwise disposed as described in the Automation project communication plan?

499. Are there contingencies or conditions related to the acceptance?

500. On budget?

501. What would the life cycle costs be?

502. Does the suggested change request seem to represent a necessary enhancement to the product?

503. Does a process exist for establishing a cost baseline to measure Automation project performance?

504. Has operations management formally accepted responsibility for operating and maintaining the product(s) or service(s) delivered by the Automation project?

505. Has the Automation project (or Automation project phase) been evaluated against each objective established in the product description and Integrated Automation project Plan?

506. Review your risk triggers -have your risks changed?

507. Has the appropriate access to relevant data and analysis capability been granted?

508. What is the consequence?

509. What is it ?

2.24 Quality Management Plan: Automation

510. What is the audience for the data?

511. Is this process still needed?

512. What changes can you make that will result in improvement?

513. What are your organizations current levels and trends for the already stated measures related to employee wellbeing, satisfaction, and development?

514. Are there procedures in place to effectively manage interdependencies with other Automation projects / systems?

515. Are there trends or hot spots?

516. Who do you send data to?

517. How are changes recorded?

518. How effectively was the Quality Management Plan applied during Automation project Execution?

519. What key performance indicators does your organization use to measure, manage, and improve key processes?

520. Does a documented Automation project organizational policy & plan (i.e. governance model)

exist?

521. What type of in-house testing do you conduct?

522. What field records are generated?

523. Are there ways to reduce the time it takes to get something approved?

524. Are there nonconformance issues?

525. How do you ensure that your sampling methods and procedures meet your data needs?

526. Who gets results of work?

527. What would you gain if you spent time working to improve this process?

2.25 Quality Metrics: Automation

528. What method of measurement do you use?

529. Were quality attributes reported?

530. Is material complete (and does it meet the standards)?

531. Was the overall quality better or worse than previous products?

532. Filter visualizations of interest?

533. Is there alignment within your organization on definitions?

534. Should a modifier be included?

535. Is a risk containment plan in place?

536. Is the reporting frequency appropriate?

537. Can visual measures help you to filter visualizations of interest?

538. How exactly do you define when differences exist?

539. How should customers provide input?

540. How do you communicate results and findings to upper management?

541. What forces exist that would cause them to change?

542. Has risk analysis been adequately reviewed?

543. Where did complaints, returns and warranty claims come from?

544. Did the team meet the Automation project success criteria documented in the Quality Metrics Matrix?

545. Are interface issues coordinated?

546. What group is empowered to define quality requirements?

547. What metrics are important and most beneficial to measure?

2.26 Process Improvement Plan: Automation

548. What actions are needed to address the problems and achieve the goals?

549. Are you meeting the quality standards?

550. Are you following the quality standards?

551. What lessons have you learned so far?

552. Are you making progress on the goals?

553. Purpose of goal: the motive is determined by asking, why do you want to achieve this goal?

554. Does explicit definition of the measures exist?

555. What personnel are the champions for the initiative?

556. Has the time line required to move measurement results from the points of collection to databases or users been established?

557. Where do you focus?

558. To elicit goal statements, do you ask a question such as, What do you want to achieve?

559. What personnel are the change agents for your initiative?

560. Management commitment at all levels?

561. Does your process ensure quality?

562. What makes people good SPI coaches?

563. Why quality management?

564. Why do you want to achieve the goal?

565. Everyone agrees on what process improvement is, right?

566. How do you manage quality?

567. Have storage and access mechanisms and procedures been determined?

2.27 Responsibility Assignment Matrix: Automation

568. Not any rs, as, or cs: if an identified role is only informed, should others be eliminated from the matrix?

569. Are all authorized tasks assigned to identified organizational elements?

570. Can the contractor substantiate work package and planning package budgets?

571. Are records maintained to show how undistributed budgets are controlled?

572. Are indirect costs accumulated for comparison with the corresponding budgets?

573. What travel needed?

574. Automation projected economic escalation?

575. Are material costs reported within the same period as that in which BCWP is earned for that material?

576. The staff characteristics – is the group or the person capable to work together as a team?

577. What is the number one predictor of a groups productivity?

578. The anticipated business volume?

579. What materials and procurements needed?

580. Evaluate the performance of operating organizations?

581. Are detailed work packages planned as far in advance as practicable?

582. Who is responsible for work and budgets for each wbs?

583. Are the wbs and organizational levels for application of the Automation projected overhead costs identified?

584. Are there any drawbacks to using a responsibility assignment matrix?

585. Are the actual costs used for variance analysis reconcilable with data from the accounting system?

2.28 Roles and Responsibilities: Automation

586. What should you do now to ensure that you are exceeding expectations and excelling in your current position?

587. Who is responsible for implementation activities and where will the functions, roles and responsibilities be defined?

588. Is the data complete?

589. Is there a training program in place for stakeholders covering expectations, roles and responsibilities and any addition knowledge others need to be good stakeholders?

590. Key conclusions and recommendations: Are conclusions and recommendations relevant and acceptable?

591. Are Automation project team roles and responsibilities identified and documented?

592. Is feedback clearly communicated and non-judgmental?

593. Who is responsible for each task?

594. Once the responsibilities are defined for the Automation project, have the deliverables, roles and responsibilities been clearly communicated to every

participant?

595. Where are you most strong as a supervisor?

596. What areas would you highlight for changes or improvements?

597. What is working well?

598. Are governance roles and responsibilities documented?

599. Are Automation project team roles and responsibilities identified and documented?

600. To decide whether to use a quality measurement, ask how will you know when it is achieved?

601. What areas of supervision are challenging for you?

602. How is your work-life balance?

603. Do the values and practices inherent in the culture of your organization foster or hinder the process?

604. What should you do now to prepare for your career 5+ years from now?

605. What should you do now to prepare yourself for a promotion, increased responsibilities or a different job?

2.29 Human Resource Management Plan: Automation

606. Does a documented Automation project organizational policy & plan (i.e. governance model) exist?

607. Has the Automation project manager been identified?

608. How are you going to ensure that you have a well motivated workforce?

609. Have activity relationships and interdependencies within tasks been adequately identified?

610. Are vendor contract reports, reviews and visits conducted periodically?

611. Are all payments made according to the contract(s)?

612. Are Automation project leaders committed to this Automation project full time?

613. Are the Automation project team members located locally to the users/stakeholders?

614. Is the current culture aligned with the vision, mission, and values of the department?

615. Have Automation project management

standards and procedures been identified / established and documented?

616. Are staff skills known and available for each task?

617. Is the Automation project schedule available for all Automation project team members to review?

618. What talent is needed?

619. Account for the purpose of this Automation project by describing, at a high-level, what will be done. What is this Automation project aiming to achieve?

620. Is there a Steering Committee in place?

621. Is it possible to track all classes of Automation project work (e.g. scheduled, un-scheduled, defect repair, etc.)?

622. Are Automation project contact logs kept up to date?

623. Is the Automation project sponsor clearly communicating the business case or rationale for why this Automation project is needed?

2.30 Communications Management Plan: Automation

624. Are there common objectives between the team and the stakeholder?

625. Do you feel more overwhelmed by stakeholders?

626. Are there too many who have an interest in some aspect of your work?

627. How do you manage communications?

628. What are the interrelationships?

629. Do you feel a register helps?

630. What steps can you take for a positive relationship?

631. What does the stakeholder need from the team?

632. How were corresponding initiatives successful?

633. Are others needed?

634. How often do you engage with stakeholders?

635. How is this initiative related to other portfolios, programs, or Automation projects?

636. What to know?

637. What is Automation project communications management?

638. Who have you worked with in past, similar initiatives?

639. Is there an important stakeholder who is actively opposed and will not receive messages?

640. Why manage stakeholders?

641. Who were proponents/opponents?

642. Which stakeholders can influence others?

2.31 Risk Management Plan: Automation

643. Can the risk be avoided by choosing a different alternative?

644. Was an original risk assessment/risk management plan completed?

645. What are the chances the event will occur?

646. Can it be changed quickly?

647. How is risk identification performed?

648. Are status updates being made on schedule and are the updates clearly described?

649. Have top software and customer managers formally committed to support the Automation project?

650. What are the cost, schedule and resource impacts of avoiding the risk?

651. Do requirements demand the use of new analysis, design, or testing methods?

652. Are end-users enthusiastically committed to the Automation project and the system/product to be built?

653. Does the customer understand the software

process?

654. What is the impact to the Automation project if the item is not resolved in a timely fashion?

655. Does the customer have a solid idea of what is required?

656. Is the customer technically sophisticated in the product area?

657. Are there risks to human health or the environment that need to be controlled or mitigated?

658. Are formal technical reviews part of this process?

659. What are some questions that should be addressed in a risk management plan?

660. Are team members trained in the use of the tools?

661. Has something like this been done before?

2.32 Risk Register: Automation

662. How could corresponding Risk affect the Automation project in terms of cost and schedule?

663. Market risk -will the new service or product be useful to your organization or marketable to others?

664. What are the assumptions and current status that support the assessment of the risk?

665. What may happen or not go according to plan?

666. What are the main aims, objectives of the policy, strategy, or service and the intended outcomes?

667. Are there any gaps in the evidence?

668. Assume the risk event or situation happens, what would the impact be?

669. How are risks identified?

670. When would you develop a risk register?

671. Who is going to do it?

672. What is a Community Risk Register?

673. Are implemented controls working as others should?

674. Manageability – have mitigations to the risk been identified?

675. What action, if any, has been taken to respond to the risk?

676. How often will the Risk Management Plan and Risk Register be formally reviewed, and by whom?

677. Having taken action, how did the responses effect change, and where is the Automation project now?

678. What would the impact to the Automation project objectives be should the risk arise?

679. What are the major risks facing the Automation project?

680. What is the probability and impact of the risk occurring?

2.33 Probability and Impact Assessment: Automation

681. What can you do about it?

682. Is there additional information that would make you more confident about your analysis?

683. How well is the risk understood?

684. Are the best people available?

685. How much is the probability of a risk occurring?

686. Supply/demand Automation projections and trends; what are the levels of accuracy?

687. Monitoring of the overall Automation project status – are there any changes in the Automation project that can effect and cause new possible risks?

688. Do the requirements require the creation of new algorithms?

689. Is security a central objective?

690. What are the current requirements of the customer?

691. Who are the international/overseas Automation project partners (equipment supplier/supplier/consultant/contractor) for this Automation project?

692. Have customers been involved fully in the definition of requirements?

693. What is the likelihood?

694. Risk may be made during which step of risk management?

695. Why has this particular mode of contracting been chosen?

696. How would you suggest monitoring for risk transition indicators?

697. Do you have a consistent repeatable process that is actually used?

698. Do you train all developers in the process?

2.34 Probability and Impact Matrix: Automation

699. Do requirements put excessive performance constraints on the product?

700. Do you manage the process through use of metrics?

701. What are the probable external agencies to act as Automation project manager?

702. Can you handle the investment risk?

703. Which phase of the Automation project do you take part in?

704. Number of users of the product?

705. What lifestyle shifts might occur in society?

706. Is the Automation project cutting across the entire organization?

707. What should be done NEXT?

708. Have top software and customer managers formally committed to support the Automation project?

709. Can the Automation project proceed without assuming the risk?

710. Do you need a risk management plan?

711. Are compilers and code generators available and suitable for the product to be built?

712. What do you expect?

713. Is the number of people on the Automation project team adequate to do the job?

714. Is the process supported by tools?

715. Are flexibility and reuse paramount?

716. Are you on schedule?

717. How risk averse are you?

2.35 Risk Data Sheet: Automation

718. What were the Causes that contributed?

719. How can hazards be reduced?

720. What are the main threats to your existence?

721. During work activities could hazards exist?

722. What do you know?

723. Is the data sufficiently specified in terms of the type of failure being analyzed, and its frequency or probability?

724. Type of risk identified?

725. Has a sensitivity analysis been carried out?

726. How can it happen?

727. What are you trying to achieve (Objectives)?

728. What if client refuses?

729. What is the chance that it will happen?

730. What is the environment within which you operate (social trends, economic, community values, broad based participation, national directions etc.)?

731. What are the main opportunities available to you that you should grab while you can?

732. What was measured?

733. Do effective diagnostic tests exist?

734. What can you do?

735. If it happens, what are the consequences?

736. What is the likelihood of it happening?

737. How do you handle product safely?

2.36 Procurement Management Plan: Automation

738. Are Automation project team members committed fulltime?

739. Have external dependencies been captured in the schedule?

740. Has a structured approach been used to break work effort into manageable components (WBS)?

741. Have stakeholder accountabilities & responsibilities been clearly defined?

742. Are the appropriate IT resources adequate to meet planned commitments?

743. Are target dates established for each milestone deliverable?

744. Are Automation project team roles and responsibilities identified and documented?

745. Is there a formal set of procedures supporting Issues Management?

746. Are the Automation project team members located locally to the users/stakeholders?

747. Has the schedule been baselined?

748. Is there a procurement management plan in

place?

749. Have all unresolved risks been documented?

750. Financial capacity; does the seller have, or can the seller reasonably be expected to obtain, the financial resources needed?

751. Staffing Requirements?

752. Has Automation project success criteria been defined?

753. Are changes in deliverable commitments agreed to by all affected groups & individuals?

754. Have Automation project team accountabilities & responsibilities been clearly defined?

2.37 Source Selection Criteria: Automation

755. What are the most common types of rating systems?

756. What are the guidelines regarding award without considerations?

757. Who should attend debriefings?

758. Are evaluators ready to begin this task?

759. Can you prevent comparison of proposals?

760. What is the role of counsel in the procurement process?

761. Is this a cost contract?

762. When is it appropriate to issue a DRFP?

763. Are considerations anticipated?

764. Do you have a plan to document consensus results including disposition of any disagreement by individual evaluators?

765. Can you make a cost/technical tradeoff?

766. Do you consider all weaknesses, significant weaknesses, and deficiencies?

767. What documentation is needed for a tradeoff decision?

768. What are the limitations on pre-competitive range communications?

769. Are there any common areas of weaknesses or deficiencies in the proposals in the competitive range?

770. What information may not be provided?

771. How do you encourage efficiency and consistency?

772. Is a cost realism analysis used?

773. Can you identify proposed teaming partners and/ or subcontractors and consider the nature and extent of proposed involvement in satisfying the Automation project requirements?

774. How are clarifications and communications appropriately used?

2.38 Stakeholder Management Plan: Automation

775. Are procurement deliverables arriving on time and to specification?

776. Have the key functions and capabilities been defined and assigned to each release or iteration?

777. Where will verification occur, and by whom?

778. How are you doing/what can be done better?

779. What specific resources will be required for implementation activities?

780. What has to be purchased?

781. Have the key elements of a coherent Automation project management strategy been established?

782. Have adequate resources been provided by management to ensure Automation project success?

783. Does all Automation project documentation reside in a common repository for easy access?

784. Who will be responsible for managing and maintaining the Issues Register?

785. Does this include subcontracted development?

786. Are milestone deliverables effectively tracked

and compared to Automation project plan?

787. Who will be collecting information?

788. How, to whom and how frequently will Risk status be reported?

789. Was your organizations estimating methodology being used and followed?

2.39 Change Management Plan: Automation

790. Has the priority for this Automation project been set by the Business Unit Management Team?

791. Has the training provider been established?

792. What risks may occur upfront, during implementation and after implementation?

793. Is there support for this application(s) and are the details available for distribution?

794. What relationships will change?

795. Who will be the change levers?

796. Impact of systems implementation on organization change?

797. Who is responsible for which tasks?

798. What risks may occur upfront?

799. Who might be able to help you the most?

800. Has the target training audience been identified and nominated?

801. Who will do the training?

802. Does this change represent a completely

new process for your organization, or a different application of an existing process?

803. What would be an estimate of the total cost for the activities required to carry out the change initiative?

804. Has a training need analysis been carried out?

805. Why is the initiative is being undertaken - What are the business drivers?

806. Have the approved procedures and policies been published?

807. When to start change management?

808. What do you expect the target audience to do, say, think or feel as a result of this communication?

809. What are the responsibilities assigned to each role?

3.0 Executing Process Group: Automation

810. How will professionals learn what is expected from them what the deliverables are?

811. Are escalated issues resolved promptly?

812. What are the critical steps involved in selecting measures and initiatives?

813. What are the main processes included in Automation project quality management?

814. What are the main types of goods and services being outsourced?

815. Why do you need a good WBS to use Automation project management software?

816. How does Automation project management relate to other disciplines?

817. It under budget or over budget?

818. How will you avoid scope creep?

819. How could stakeholders negatively impact your Automation project?

820. Why is it important to determine activity sequencing on Automation projects?

821. Is the Automation project performing better or worse than planned?

822. Mitigate. what will you do to minimize the impact should a risk event occur?

823. What are crucial elements of successful Automation project plan execution?

824. Is the schedule for the set products being met?

825. Do the products created live up to the necessary quality?

826. Do schedule issues conflicts?

827. What are deliverables of your Automation project?

828. Who will be the main sponsor?

829. What are some crucial elements of a good Automation project plan?

3.1 Team Member Status Report: Automation

830. Does your organization have the means (staff, money, contract, etc.) to produce or to acquire the product, good, or service?

831. Are the attitudes of staff regarding Automation project work improving?

832. What specific interest groups do you have in place?

833. Will the staff do training or is that done by a third party?

834. Are the products of your organizations Automation projects meeting customers objectives?

835. How can you make it practical?

836. How does this product, good, or service meet the needs of the Automation project and your organization as a whole?

837. Are your organizations Automation projects more successful over time?

838. What is to be done?

839. How it is to be done?

840. Does the product, good, or service already exist

within your organization?

841. When a teams productivity and success depend on collaboration and the efficient flow of information, what generally fails them?

842. The problem with Reward & Recognition Programs is that the truly deserving people all too often get left out. How can you make it practical?

843. Why is it to be done?

844. Do you have an Enterprise Automation project Management Office (EPMO)?

845. How will resource planning be done?

846. How much risk is involved?

847. Is there evidence that staff is taking a more professional approach toward management of your organizations Automation projects?

848. Does every department have to have a Automation project Manager on staff?

3.2 Change Request: Automation

849. Will there be a change request form in use?

850. Has a formal technical review been conducted to assess technical correctness?

851. Will new change requests be acknowledged in a timely manner?

852. Will the change use memory to the extent that other functions will be not have sufficient memory to operate effectively?

853. Are there requirements attributes that can discriminate between high and low reliability?

854. Should a more thorough impact analysis be conducted?

855. What are the basic mechanics of the Change Advisory Board (CAB)?

856. What needs to be communicated?

857. Are there requirements attributes that are strongly related to the occurrence of defects and failures?

858. How is quality being addressed on the Automation project?

859. Since there are no change requests in your Automation project at this point, what must you have

before you begin?

860. Is it feasible to use requirements attributes as predictors of reliability?

861. What is the relationship between requirements attributes and reliability?

862. What are the duties of the change control team?

863. How many lines of code must be changed to implement the change?

864. What are the Impacts to your organization?

865. Who is communicating the change?

866. When to submit a change request?

867. What mechanism is used to appraise others of changes that are made?

868. Has the change been highlighted and documented in the CSCI?

3.3 Change Log: Automation

869. Is the change request within Automation project scope?

870. Is this a mandatory replacement?

871. Is the change backward compatible without limitations?

872. Will the Automation project fail if the change request is not executed?

873. Who initiated the change request?

874. When was the request submitted?

875. Is the change request open, closed or pending?

876. How does this change affect the timeline of the schedule?

877. When was the request approved?

878. Is the requested change request a result of changes in other Automation project(s)?

879. How does this change affect scope?

880. Is the submitted change a new change or a modification of a previously approved change?

881. Do the described changes impact on the integrity or security of the system?

882. How does this relate to the standards developed for specific business processes?

883. Does the suggested change request represent a desired enhancement to the products functionality?

884. Where do changes come from?

3.4 Decision Log: Automation

885. Decision-making process; how will the team make decisions?

886. Who will be given a copy of this document and where will it be kept?

887. What is the average size of your matters in an applicable measurement?

888. How do you know when you are achieving it?

889. Who is the decisionmaker?

890. How consolidated and comprehensive a story can you tell by capturing currently available incident data in a central location and through a log of key decisions during an incident?

891. Does anything need to be adjusted?

892. Adversarial environment. is your opponent open to a non-traditional workflow, or will it likely challenge anything you do?

893. How does the use a Decision Support System influence the strategies/tactics or costs?

894. What is the line where eDiscovery ends and document review begins?

895. What makes you different or better than others companies selling the same thing?

896. With whom was the decision shared or considered?

897. How does an increasing emphasis on cost containment influence the strategies and tactics used?

898. How do you define success?

899. What is your overall strategy for quality control / quality assurance procedures?

900. How does provision of information, both in terms of content and presentation, influence acceptance of alternative strategies?

901. Meeting purpose; why does this team meet?

902. It becomes critical to track and periodically revisit both operational effectiveness; Are you noticing all that you need to, and are you interpreting what you see effectively?

903. At what point in time does loss become unacceptable?

904. Which variables make a critical difference?

3.5 Quality Audit: Automation

905. How does your organization know that it is appropriately effective and constructive in preparing its staff for organizational aspirations?

906. How does your organization know that its system for inducting new staff to maximize workplace contributions are appropriately effective and constructive?

907. How do you know what, specifically, is required of you in your work?

908. How does your organization know that its Strategic Plan is providing the best guidance for the future of your organization?

909. What has changed/improved as a result of the review processes?

910. How does your organization know that its quality of teaching is appropriately effective and constructive?

911. How does your organization know that its systems for meeting staff extracurricular learning support requirements are appropriately effective and constructive?

912. Are people allowed to contribute ideas?

913. How does your organization know that its risk management system is appropriately effective and

constructive?

914. How does your organization know that its teaching activities (and staff learning) are effectively and constructively enhanced by its activities?

915. How does your organization know that its system for ensuring that its training activities are appropriately resourced and support is appropriately effective and constructive?

916. How does your organization know that the range and quality of its social and recreational services and facilities are appropriately effective and constructive in meeting the needs of staff?

917. How does your organization know that the support for its staff is appropriately effective and constructive?

918. Are all areas associated with the storage and reconditioning of devices clean, free of rubbish, adequately ventilated and in good repair?

919. How does your organization know that its system for attending to the particular needs of its international staff is appropriately effective and constructive?

920. Does the suppliers quality system have a written procedure for corrective action when a defect occurs?

921. How does your organization know that its financial management system is appropriately effective and constructive?

922. How does the organization know that its industry and community engagement planning and management systems are appropriately effective and constructive in enabling relationships with key stakeholder groups?

923. Is quality audit a prerequisite for program accreditation or program recognition?

924. Are training programs documented?

3.6 Team Directory: Automation

925. Process decisions: do job conditions warrant additional actions to collect job information and document on-site activity?

926. Decisions: is the most suitable form of contract being used?

927. Who will write the meeting minutes and distribute?

928. Timing: when do the effects of communication take place?

929. How does the team resolve conflicts and ensure tasks are completed?

930. Who will report Automation project status to all stakeholders?

931. Where should the information be distributed?

932. What are you going to deliver or accomplish?

933. Does a Automation project team directory list all resources assigned to the Automation project?

934. How do unidentified risks impact the outcome of the Automation project?

935. How and in what format should information be presented?

936. Who are your stakeholders (customers, sponsors, end users, team members)?

937. Decisions: what could be done better to improve the quality of the constructed product?

938. Is construction on schedule?

939. Why is the work necessary?

940. When does information need to be distributed?

941. Process decisions: is work progressing on schedule and per contract requirements?

942. Days from the time the issue is identified?

3.7 Team Operating Agreement: Automation

943. What is a Virtual Team?

944. Are team roles clearly defined and accepted?

945. To whom do you deliver your services?

946. How will group handle unplanned absences?

947. Do you solicit member feedback about meetings and what would make them better?

948. Have you established procedures that team members can follow to work effectively together, such as a team operating agreement?

949. How will your group handle planned absences?

950. Reimbursements: how will the team members be reimbursed for expenses and time commitments?

951. How will you divide work equitably?

952. Are there differences in access to communication and collaboration technology based on team member location?

953. Confidentiality: how will confidential information be handled?

954. Did you delegate tasks such as taking meeting

minutes, presenting a topic and soliciting input?

955. Did you determine the technology methods that best match the messages to be communicated?

956. Must your members collaborate successfully to complete Automation projects?

957. What are the boundaries (organizational or geographic) within which you operate?

958. Do you ask participants to close laptops and place mobile devices on silent on the table while the meeting is in progress?

959. Do you post meeting notes and the recording (if used) and notify participants?

960. Do you post any action items, due dates, and responsibilities on the team website?

961. What are some potential sources of conflict among team members?

3.8 Team Performance Assessment: Automation

962. To what degree does the teams work approach provide opportunity for members to engage in fact-based problem solving?

963. To what degree does the teams approach to its work allow for modification and improvement over time?

964. Lack of method variance in self-reported affect and perceptions at work: Reality or artifact?

965. To what degree does the teams purpose constitute a broader, deeper aspiration than just accomplishing short-term goals?

966. To what degree are sub-teams possible or necessary?

967. Which situations call for a more extreme type of adaptiveness in which team members actually re-define roles?

968. What do you think is the most constructive thing that could be done now to resolve considerations and disputes about method variance?

969. Can familiarity breed backup?

970. Is there a particular method of data analysis that you would recommend as a means of demonstrating

that method variance is not of great concern for a given dataset?

971. To what degree are the members clear on what they are individually responsible for and what they are jointly responsible for?

972. To what degree does the teams purpose contain themes that are particularly meaningful and memorable?

973. To what degree will new and supplemental skills be introduced as the need is recognized?

974. To what degree can team members vigorously define the teams purpose in considerations with others who are not part of the functioning team?

975. When a reviewer complains about method variance, what is the essence of the complaint?

976. To what degree will the approach capitalize on and enhance the skills of all team members in a manner that takes into consideration other demands on members of the team?

977. What are teams?

978. To what degree are corresponding categories of skills either actually or potentially represented across the membership?

979. If you are worried about method variance before you collect data, what sort of design elements might you include to reduce or eliminate the threat of method variance?

980. To what degree do team members feel that the purpose of the team is important, if not exciting?

981. To what degree can the team measure progress against specific goals?

3.9 Team Member Performance Assessment: Automation

982. How do you start collaborating?

983. Are any validation activities performed?

984. How accurately is your plan implemented?

985. Why do performance reviews?

986. What are the staffs preferences for training on technology-based platforms?

987. To what degree do members articulate the goals beyond the team membership?

988. What is a general description of the processes under performance measurement and assessment?

989. Are the goals SMART ?

990. What, if any, steps are available for employees who feel they have been unfairly or inaccurately rated?

991. What innovations (if any) are developed to realize goals?

992. Is it clear how goals will be accomplished?

993. What resources do you need?

994. To what degree do team members understand one anothers roles and skills?

995. How do you make use of research?

996. How is your organizations Strategic Management System tied to performance measurement?

997. How are training activities developed from a technical perspective?

998. How do you determine which data are the most important to use, analyze, or review?

999. How are performance measures and associated incentives developed?

3.10 Issue Log: Automation

1000. What is the impact on the risks?

1001. Why not more evaluators?

1002. Can an impact cause deviation beyond team, stage or Automation project tolerances?

1003. Persistence; will users learn a work around or will they be bothered every time?

1004. What is the stakeholders political influence?

1005. Do you have members of your team responsible for certain stakeholders?

1006. How do you reply to this question; you am new here and managing this major program. How do you suggest you build your network?

1007. What is a Stakeholder?

1008. Why multiple evaluators?

1009. What is the status of the issue?

1010. Are the Automation project issues uniquely identified, including to which product they refer?

1011. In your work, how much time is spent on stakeholder identification?

1012. How were past initiatives successful?

1013. What would have to change?

4.0 Monitoring and Controlling Process Group: Automation

1014. Accuracy: what design will lead to accurate information?

1015. Where is the Risk in the Automation project?

1016. When will the Automation project be done?

1017. Are the services being delivered?

1018. Does the solution fit in with organizations technical architectural requirements?

1019. What kinds of things in particular are you looking for data on?

1020. How should needs be met?

1021. How was the program set-up initiated?

1022. What business situation is being addressed?

1023. What resources (both financial and non-financial) are available/needed?

1024. Is the verbiage used appropriate and understandable?

1025. Key stakeholders to work with. How many potential communications channels exist on the Automation project?

1026. What do they need to know about the Automation project?

1027. Use: how will they use the information?

1028. Did the Automation project team have the right skills?

1029. What is the timeline?

4.1 Project Performance Report: Automation

1030. To what degree do all members feel responsible for all agreed-upon measures?

1031. What degree are the relative importance and priority of the goals clear to all team members?

1032. What is in it for you?

1033. To what degree are the structures of the formal organization consistent with the behaviors in the informal organization?

1034. How is the data used?

1035. To what degree do team members articulate the teams work approach?

1036. To what degree does the teams work approach provide opportunity for members to engage in results-based evaluation?

1037. To what degree do the goals specify concrete team work products?

1038. To what degree does the team possess adequate membership to achieve its ends?

1039. How will procurement be coordinated with other Automation project aspects, such as scheduling and performance reporting?

1040. To what degree do individual skills and abilities match task demands?

1041. To what degree will the team ensure that all members equitably share the work essential to the success of the team?

1042. To what degree are the skill areas critical to team performance present?

1043. To what degree do team members frequently explore the teams purpose and its implications?

1044. To what degree can the team ensure that all members are individually and jointly accountable for the teams purpose, goals, approach, and work-products?

4.2 Variance Analysis: Automation

1045. Are work packages assigned to performing organizations?

1046. What is the budgeted cost for work scheduled?

1047. Can the relationship with problem customers be restructured so that there is a win-win situation?

1048. Did an existing competitor change strategy?

1049. Can process improvements lead to unfavorable variances?

1050. How are material, labor, and overhead variances calculated and recorded?

1051. What business event causes fluctuations?

1052. Does the contractors system identify work accomplishment against the schedule plan?

1053. Why are standard cost systems used?

1054. Budgeted cost for work performed?

1055. Does the contractors system provide unit or lot costs when applicable?

1056. Favorable or unfavorable variance?

1057. What causes selling price variance?

1058. Are all cwbs elements specified for external reporting?

1059. How do you identify potential or actual overruns and underruns?

1060. Are overhead costs budgets established on a basis consistent with the anticipated direct business base?

1061. Are indirect costs charged to the appropriate indirect pools and incurring organization?

1062. Are significant decision points, constraints, and interfaces identified as key milestones?

4.3 Earned Value Status: Automation

1063. Are you hitting your Automation projects targets?

1064. How much is it going to cost by the finish?

1065. What is the unit of forecast value?

1066. If earned value management (EVM) is so good in determining the true status of a Automation project and Automation project its completion, why is it that hardly any one uses it in information systems related Automation projects?

1067. When is it going to finish?

1068. Validation is a process of ensuring that the developed system will actually achieve the stakeholders desired outcomes; Are you building the right product? What do you validate?

1069. Earned value can be used in almost any Automation project situation and in almost any Automation project environment. it may be used on large Automation projects, medium sized Automation projects, tiny Automation projects (in cut-down form), complex and simple Automation projects and in any market sector. some people, of course, know all about earned value, they have used it for years - but perhaps not as effectively as they could have?

1070. Where is evidence-based earned value in your organization reported?

1071. Verification is a process of ensuring that the developed system satisfies the stakeholders agreements and specifications; Are you building the product right? What do you verify?

1072. How does this compare with other Automation projects?

1073. Where are your problem areas?

4.4 Risk Audit: Automation

1074. Does your organization meet the terms of any contracts with which it is involved?

1075. Do you record and file all audits?

1076. Do you have financial policies and procedures in place to guide officers of your organization/treasurer/general members?

1077. Estimated size of product in number of programs, files, transactions?

1078. Are your rules, by-laws and practices non-discriminatory?

1079. What does internal control mean in the context of the audit process?

1080. Does the adoption of a business risk audit approach change internal control documentation and testing practices?

1081. What are the costs associated with late delivery or a defective product?

1082. Is the customer willing to participate in reviews?

1083. Tradeoff: how much risk can be tolerated and still deliver the products where they need to be?

1084. Have all possible risks/hazards been identified (including injury to staff, damage to equipment, impact on others in the community)?

1085. How do you manage risk?

1086. What are the outcomes you are looking for?

1087. Is all required equipment available?

1088. Has an event time line been developed?

1089. Are testing tools available and suitable?

4.5 Contractor Status Report: Automation

1090. What process manages the contracts?

1091. Describe how often regular updates are made to the proposed solution. Are corresponding regular updates included in the standard maintenance plan?

1092. What are the minimum and optimal bandwidth requirements for the proposed soluiton?

1093. Are there contractual transfer concerns?

1094. How does the proposed individual meet each requirement?

1095. Who can list a Automation project as organization experience, your organization or a previous employee of your organization?

1096. If applicable; describe your standard schedule for new software version releases. Are new software version releases included in the standard maintenance plan?

1097. How is risk transferred?

1098. What was the final actual cost?

1099. What was the actual budget or estimated cost for your organizations services?

1100. What is the average response time for answering a support call?

1101. How long have you been using the services?

1102. What was the overall budget or estimated cost?

1103. What was the budget or estimated cost for your organizations services?

4.6 Formal Acceptance: Automation

1104. What are the requirements against which to test, Who will execute?

1105. Was the client satisfied with the Automation project results?

1106. Was the Automation project work done on time, within budget, and according to specification?

1107. Was the Automation project goal achieved?

1108. Who supplies data?

1109. What can you do better next time?

1110. How well did the team follow the methodology?

1111. General estimate of the costs and times to complete the Automation project?

1112. Is formal acceptance of the Automation project product documented and distributed?

1113. What features, practices, and processes proved to be strengths or weaknesses?

1114. Does it do what Automation project team said it would?

1115. What is the Acceptance Management Process?

1116. Who would use it?

1117. Was the Automation project managed well?

1118. What lessons were learned about your Automation project management methodology?

1119. How does your team plan to obtain formal acceptance on your Automation project?

1120. Did the Automation project manager and team act in a professional and ethical manner?

1121. Do you buy pre-configured systems or build your own configuration?

1122. Do you perform formal acceptance or burn-in tests?

1123. Have all comments been addressed?

5.0 Closing Process Group: Automation

1124. Are there funding or time constraints?

1125. Was the schedule met?

1126. Did the Automation project management methodology work?

1127. What communication items need improvement?

1128. How will staff learn how to use the deliverables?

1129. Is this a follow-on to a previous Automation project?

1130. When will the Automation project be done?

1131. Specific - is the objective clear in terms of what, how, when, and where the situation will be changed?

1132. How well did the team follow the chosen processes?

1133. How will you know you did it?

1134. How critical is the Automation project success to the success of your organization?

1135. Were sponsors and decision makers available when needed outside regularly scheduled meetings?

1136. Can the lesson learned be replicated?

1137. Did you do what you said you were going to do?

1138. If action is called for, what form should it take?

1139. What is the Automation project name and date of completion?

1140. What areas were overlooked on this Automation project?

1141. What level of risk does the proposed budget represent to the Automation project?

1142. What is the Automation project Management Process?

5.1 Procurement Audit: Automation

1143. Are obtained prices/qualities competitive to prices/qualities obtained by other procurement functions/units, comparing obtained or improved value for money?

1144. Were no tenders presented after the time limit accepted?

1145. Is there a legal authority for the procurement Automation project?

1146. Was a sufficient competitive environment created?

1147. Did your organization state the minimum requirements to be met by the variants in the tender documents?

1148. Are the official minutes written in a clear and concise manner?

1149. Is the appropriate procurement approach being chosen (considering for example the possibility of contracting out work or procuring low value items through a specific low cost procuring system)?

1150. Are there mechanisms in place to evaluate the performance of the departments suppliers?

1151. Does the procurement Automation project have a clear goal and does the goal meet the specified needs of the users?

1152. Are unsuccessful companies informed why tender failed?

1153. Did your organization decide for an appropriate and admissible procurement procedure?

1154. Is your organization policy on purchasing covered by a written manual?

1155. Was the pre-qualification screening for issue of tender documents done properly and in a fair manner?

1156. Months to reflect any changes in policy?

1157. Did the bidder comply with requests within the deadline set?

1158. Has your organization procedures in place to monitor the input of experts employed to assist the procurement function?

1159. Are all initial purchase contracts made by the purchasing organization?

1160. Are approval limits definitive as to amount and classification of expenditure?

1161. Are petty cash funds operated on an imprest basis?

1162. Are procedures established on how orders will be shipped?

5.2 Contract Close-Out: Automation

1163. Change in knowledge?

1164. What is capture management?

1165. Have all contract records been included in the Automation project archives?

1166. Was the contract sufficiently clear so as not to result in numerous disputes and misunderstandings?

1167. Parties: who is involved?

1168. Change in circumstances?

1169. How/when used ?

1170. Has each contract been audited to verify acceptance and delivery?

1171. Was the contract complete without requiring numerous changes and revisions?

1172. Have all contracts been completed?

1173. Are the signers the authorized officials?

1174. What happens to the recipient of services?

1175. Have all contracts been closed?

1176. Was the contract type appropriate?

1177. Why Outsource?

1178. How is the contracting office notified of the automatic contract close-out?

1179. Change in attitude or behavior?

1180. How does it work?

1181. Have all acceptance criteria been met prior to final payment to contractors?

1182. Parties: Authorized?

5.3 Project or Phase Close-Out: Automation

1183. Planned remaining costs?

1184. Were cost budgets met?

1185. What security considerations needed to be addressed during the procurement life cycle?

1186. What were the desired outcomes?

1187. Who controlled the resources for the Automation project?

1188. Were the outcomes different from the already stated planned?

1189. When and how were information needs best met?

1190. What are they?

1191. Planned completion date?

1192. Have business partners been involved extensively, and what data was required for them?

1193. What are the informational communication needs for each stakeholder?

1194. If you were the Automation project sponsor, how would you determine which Automation project team(s) and/or individuals deserve recognition?

1195. What process was planned for managing issues/ risks?

1196. Did the delivered product meet the specified requirements and goals of the Automation project?

1197. What could have been improved?

1198. What information did each stakeholder need to contribute to the Automation projects success?

1199. What benefits or impacts does the stakeholder group expect to obtain as a result of the Automation project?

1200. What could be done to improve the process?

1201. Were messages directly related to the release strategy or phases of the Automation project?

5.4 Lessons Learned: Automation

1202. How closely did deliverables match what was defined within the Automation project Scope?

1203. Was there enough support – guidance, clerical support, training?

1204. How effective was the documentation that you received with the Automation project product/service?

1205. How effective was the quality assurance process?

1206. How useful and complete was the Automation project document repository?

1207. How clearly defined were the objectives for this Automation project?

1208. What was the methodology behind successful learning experiences, and how might they be applied to the broader challenge of your organizations knowledge management?

1209. What on the Automation project worked well and was effective in the delivery of the product?

1210. How many government and contractor personnel are authorized for the Automation project?

1211. How effective were the communications materials in providing and orienting team members about the details of the Automation project?

1212. What were the problems encountered in the Automation project-functional area relationship, why, and how could they be fixed?

1213. How well did the scope of the Automation project match what was defined in the Automation project Proposal?

1214. Is the lesson significant, valid, and applicable?

1215. Is your organization willing to expose problems or mistakes for the betterment of the collective whole, and can you do this in a way that does not intimidate employees or workers?

1216. How efficient and effective were Automation project team meetings?

1217. What regulatory regime controlled how your organization head and program manager directed your organization and Automation project?

1218. How much flexibility is there in the funding (e.g., what authorities does the program manager have to change to the specifics of the funding within the overall funding ceiling)?

1219. Who needs to learn lessons?

1220. How well do you feel the executives supported this Automation project?

1221. Was the Automation project significantly delayed/hampered by outside dependencies (outside to the Automation project, that is)?

Index

293

procedure   101, 112, 233, 263
procedures   11, 28, 52, 71, 74, 81-82, 89-90, 128, 131, 146, 163,
172, 182, 190-191, 195, 201, 214, 221, 231, 237, 254, 263
proceed   210
proceeding   179-180
process   1-7, 11, 21, 28, 30-31, 33, 36, 39-45, 47-66, 73-75,
79, 82-90, 93, 95, 97-102, 105-107, 111-115, 118-121, 123-124,
126-127, 129-130, 135-136, 142, 147-149, 152-154, 162, 172, 177-
178, 185, 189-191, 194-195, 199, 205, 209-211, 216, 221-222, 230,
235-236, 246, 250, 252-254, 256, 258, 260-261, 267-268
processed   57, 60
processes   35, 40, 49-50, 52, 54-58, 60-66, 83, 86, 93, 97, 103-
104, 106, 113, 115-116, 118, 122, 125, 135, 147, 156-157, 190, 222,
229, 232, 242, 258, 260
processing   52, 56
procuring   262
produce   70, 100, 131, 135, 172, 184, 224
produced   44
produces   167
producing   152
product   1, 11, 45, 64-65, 102, 112, 119, 123, 128, 130, 146,
148, 154-156, 169, 176, 188-189, 204-206, 210-211, 213, 224, 236,
244, 252-254, 258, 267-268
production   22, 46, 60, 88, 94, 102, 105-106, 157
productive   116
products   1, 78, 111, 118, 129, 142, 152, 160, 192, 223-224,
229, 248, 254
profession   124
profit   52
program   21, 44, 53, 71, 73, 103, 142, 198, 234, 244, 246,
269
programs   68, 202, 225, 234, 254
progress   29, 56, 114, 136, 142-143, 186, 194, 238, 241
project 2-7, 9, 23, 29, 42, 45, 78, 81, 90, 110, 134-149, 152, 154-
159, 163-166, 168, 170-171, 176-190, 193, 198-201, 203-208, 210-
211, 214-215, 217-220, 222-226, 228, 235, 244, 246-248, 252, 256,
258-262, 264, 266-270
projected   196-197
projects   2, 42, 44, 78, 97, 134, 137, 140, 142-143, 152, 154,
158, 190, 202, 222, 224-225, 238, 252-253, 267
promote   141
promotion   45, 199
promptly   136, 222

CPSIA information can be obtained
at www.ICGtesting.com
Printed in the USA
BVHW080803220419

546159BV00025B/1683/P

9 780655 541240